THE
ARTIST'S
ROADMAP

NAVIGATING YOUR CAREER
IN **SHOW** BUSINESS

RICHARD LAWSON

LEGACY
launch pad
PUBLISHING

ISBN: 978-1-964377-71-1 (paperback)

ISBN: 978-1-964377-73-5 (ebook)

ISBN: 978-1-964377-77-3 (hardcover)

Dedication & Memoriam

In memory of:

*My mother, Gertie Broussard Lawson, and my sister,
Gwendolyn Ann Lawson*

My mentors, Milton Katselas and Sonny Jim Gaines

Table of Contents

TABLE OF CONTENTS

Preface

On March 7, 1969, I was cast in my first production as an actor, a musical called *Golden Boy*. I played the lead part of Joe Wellington, and on closing night we sang the final song, "I Ain't Bowin' Down." Right in the middle of it, I was thunderstruck with an epiphany that this is what God put me on this earth to do. I suddenly became conscious of something greater than myself.

While I was having this elevated and illuminating moment with God, I didn't realize I had stopped singing. One of my castmates tapped me on my shoulder and sternly whispered, "*I ain't bowin' down.*" I returned to the present, faced the audience, and sang like I'd never sung before.

From that moment to this day, I've been on vacation. My life, for the most part, has been incredibly fulfilling because my purpose has been my North Star. That's not to say that the road has been smooth and easy. It has been the wildest roller coaster ride imaginable, but being connected to my purpose has given me a GPS that has kept me moving forward, even though there has been a lot of rerouting during the process.

Early on in life, I recognized that the things I do really well are guide, support and empower individuals to realize their aspirations. One of my students called me a "dream weaver." I thought about it and decided that I could totally receive that gracious designation. I see it as a metaphor that represents my work with people to clarify their objectives and align their goals with their core values and priorities, all while mentoring them to devise a detailed action plan that includes clear milestones and outcomes.

One of the most satisfying experiences I've ever had as a dream weaver happened while screening my film *Black Terror* at the Cannes Film Festival. Two of my students were also screening films at the festival—they had made the films while in my class. Yes, I am blessed to know why I am on this planet. It's to be that dream weaver.

From 1983 to 1994, I was the key component in helping administrate and run the drug education, training, treatment and aftercare program for the National Basketball Association/ National Basketball Players Association. I say "key" because all the players knew me from my work as an actor, so even though I was with them on official business as a drug counselor, I didn't represent a suit looking to catch them in nefarious activities. They trusted me.

I trained under Dr. Dave Lewis, Kip Flock and John Bradshaw, three of the top men in their field. I was instrumental in helping to make that program one of the most successful drug programs in corporate America.

On March 22, 1992, I was on US Air's flight 405, which crashed during takeoff from New York's LaGuardia Airport. 27 people died, and 24 people survived. An event of this magnitude indelibly affects your psyche and spirit. It teaches you that there are no guarantees in life. You have to live every day as if it's your last.

I've had the pleasure of being a teacher for over 40 years. I was very fortunate to have been mentored by arguably one of the best acting teachers in the world, Milton Katselas. One of the most incredible and meaningful things I've received from anybody was a note he wrote after directing me in the play *Streamers*.

Dear Richard,

You are one of the main reasons I believe in my Teaching. You are Tops. An explorative, courageous, risky, artist. I'd love us to work together again soon. and then again. I wish you all Success. love.

Milton

I became Milton's protégé *(a person who is guided and mentored by someone with more experience in a particular field or area)*. I taught all of his classes, including his master classes. The list of people he taught was a who's who in the industry, including, James Cromwell, Burt Reynolds, John Glover, George Clooney, Kate Hudson, Michelle Pfeiffer, Doris Roberts, Jenna Elfman, Giovanni Ribisi, Tom Selleck, Tony Danza, Jeffrey Tambor, Lakshmi Manchu, Anne Archer, Robert Urich, Patrick Swayze, Michael Peña to name a few.

I was also lucky enough to have an excellent manager, Ron Muchnick. We realized early on that if we wanted it, we would have to go and get it. So that's what we did. We produced our own productions. We didn't wait for things to come to us. Together, we made things happen.

One of the things I learned from teaching people who had achieved a high level of success was that they weren't always the most talented actors in those classes. But their passion, their work ethic, the way they leaned into the teaching, the way they let the teacher talk into their ear, the clarity of the vision they had for themselves and their strategic abilities—the way they handled what I call their "Career Bus"—put them on a path destined for success.

At a certain point, given what I learned from my mentor and my experience as a consistently working actor, I began to develop my own unique style and approach. Over time, I developed my teaching philosophy. I learned that it wasn't enough to just be a good actor. You must have a good business mind to succeed in Show Business.

When I look back throughout my life and consider the journey that I've been on as an artist, which started during the Blaxploitation period, I can't tell you how grateful I am to be able to use my talents to help make the world a better place. Because I am a teacher, I am blessed to help other artists find their truth and develop their sense of responsibility and contribution to our planet. There is something incredibly noble and beautiful about what we do.

Dreams

Hold fast to dreams
For if dreams die
Life is a broken-winged bird
That cannot fly.

Hold fast to dreams
For when dreams go
Life is a barren field
Frozen with snow.

~ Langston Hughes

Dreams Don't Have Expiration Dates

To Dream

Most of us have big dreams. Sometimes, they are fantastical. Other times, they're complicated and dense with many parts. Often, they're colorful and imaginative—even otherworldly. Occasionally, our dreams frighten us. Sometimes, we wonder, who are we to even think such a thing? How dare we be so bold and arrogant? How could we be so selfish to think about ourselves, and not think about others first?

When you're on an airplane and the oxygen mask drops in front of you, the instructions are to put your mask on first so that you can help others. Otherwise, you will perish.

If you are bold and courageous enough to lock into that spectacular vision, you will be able to put your head down and carry out the mundane tasks, checking off action items that will lead you to achieve your goals.

Dream It

Everything in life is an invention that started with somebody's dream. Every car, house, streetlight, writing pen, desk, airplane and anything you can imagine started with someone dreaming it up. You dream your families up. You dream your life up. You don't always get there because somewhere along the way, someone or something will talk you out of it. You will go into agreement with someone else's loss or someone else's suppression of your ideas, dreams, or concepts. You go into agreement with the naysayers, pessimists, haters, doubters and distractors.

Don't be afraid to follow your first mind, your first thought, because that is your genius. What is true for you *is true*. Be extravagant with your imagination. If you had a dream way back when, resurrect it. Pull it out and rehabilitate it. Dress it up and give it a go. It's never too late to follow your dream.

See It

When Thomas Edison was trying to figure out the puzzle of sustainable light, he turned to Lewis Latimer, a brilliant Black man, who gave him the keys to how to do it. Latimer also helped Alexander Graham Bell invent the telephone.

These men visualized the things they would eventually create. They saw it in their minds. They did the mental repetitions over and over again, much like how great athletes will practice the shot thousands of times a day. They simulate the game-winning moments so that they just repeat the process on the night. In the end, it's déjà vu. It's happening for a second time, because the first was when you saw it in your mind.

Believe It

When you're talking about dreams, one of the biggest challenges is getting past your fear. I'm here to tell you, don't be afraid of how big your dream is. Let it be as big as it is. You will figure it out. You can't and won't do it all at once. You will do it in phases.

A developer buys 5,000 acres of land and is going to build 2,000 homes. They're not going to build 2,000 homes at once. They will phase it in. Build 25 at a time. Sell the first lot while the second is being built, and the foundation is being poured into the third. It's a process with a clear plan of execution. You have to have a strong reality about the dream. When I was a kid, I dreamed about being a jockey. I loved horses. However, by the time I was 13, I was way too big to be a jockey. But I could have been a trainer or owner.

Tell It

I created something called the Declaration of Independence, or DOIN. Ultimately, it's a blueprint for your life and career. To declare something is to make it known. Blast it out. Announce it to the world. Claim it. Proclaim it, just like a proud parent of a newborn does. Sometimes, frankly, they can get on your nerves with their proclamations of their new child. They are proud of that child, and rightfully so. The same has to happen when you give birth to your "dream" child. When parents do that, it makes them accountable. When you do that with your baby, it makes you accountable. It forces you to step up and finish it, especially if you have an accountability group as a part of your community.

Plan It

Prior Planning Prevents Poor Performance. Everything requires a plan. If you don't make a plan and carry it through daily, you will gradually get disappointed, frustrated, disillusioned and ultimately depressed. With a plan, you stay focused on your goals and raison d'être *(purpose)*. You stay on point, pursuing your dream with a sense of urgency and enthusiasm. You live in abundance, not scarcity.

Work It

As it says in The Book of James, 2:14-17:

> *What good is it, my brothers, if someone says he has faith but does not have works? Can that faith save him? If a brother or sister is poorly clothed and lacking in daily food, and one of you says to them, 'Go in peace, be warmed and filled,' without giving them the things needed for the body, what good is that? So also faith by itself, if it does not have works, is dead.*

This wild and crazy dream of yours requires your undivided attention. It requires hard work, commitment, undying faith and unwavering effort. If you have seen your dream and believe in it, you will face the storm and rage against the whole cry of voices on the other side with good-humored inflexibility until you experience the sense of déjà vu you know is yours to have. Of course, there is a little madness involved in this.

Ceremony of Respect

When you are on a journey of manifesting your dream and are clear about the result, you must have ceremonies of respect to acknowledge the process. You must honor the experience, the good times and the challenges. Of course, *There Are No Losses, Only Lessons.* In my school, we dance before and at the end of each class. We are consistent about honoring the process. It is what keeps you in the game. It's a level of gratitude that must be maintained and respected.

In my classes, the very first thing we do is have someone write up their DOIN (Declaration of Independence, aka business plan; see page 263 for details). I'm interested in what a person's dream is. What is their purpose? It's important to determine why a person is here. If I understand that, I can help them chart the course to help them accomplish that vision. Without that GPS, which the purpose provides, we are on an adventure with no specific destination, as opposed to a clear, intentional and purpose-filled journey.

Precepts

Precept:
1. A general rule to empower imagination and understanding.

When I look back over the 55+ years of pursuing my passion as an artist, and I think about the roller coaster ride it has been, a strong set of precepts have been the cornerstones to keep me grounded and in the game. They support my teachings, beliefs and way of life. These precepts help build strength and character and provide guidance, especially during challenging times.

It's essential to choose precepts that resonate with you. So, while these behavioral principles can be powerful tools, they are most effective when used as a part of a broader strategy of self-improvement and goal attainment.

- *Space Where Art Can Occur*

    The proper conditions must be in place for something to grow or realize its full potential.

- *Never Let Your Creativity Pass Through the Lens of Someone Else's Morality*

    You must protect your creative process from the judgment of others.

- *Passion Fuels Progress*

    Having passion is your key to the kingdom.

- ***You Can't Teach Through a Frown***

  An openness to receiving your lessons will shorten your trip.

- ***Make It Go Right***

  You will have greater control of your destiny.

- ***There Are No Losses, Only Lessons***

  A lesson in turning manure into fertilizer.

- ***Radical Remission***

  Taking radical control changes your condition.

- ***Career Bus***

  Handling the people and things that affect your life and career.

- ***Relationship Map***

  All the people you know and how you engage with them.

- ***Outflow Equals Inflow***

  The energy you put out equals the energy that comes back.

- ***12 Hours of Light and 12 Hours of Darkness***

  This is the balance between your assets and liabilities.

- ***We Are Only as Sick as Our Biggest Secret***

  Our greatest obstacles are hidden behind our biggest secrets.

- ***Guilt is "I Made A Mistake." Shame is "I Am A Mistake"***

  Deal with it during the guilt stage before it gets to shame.

- ***Freedom Is Having Nothing to Hide***

  Transparency allows you to be fully present.

- ***Acting Is Standing Up Naked and Turning Around Very Slowly***

  This is the sister precept to ***Freedom is Having Nothing to Hide***.

- ***Ask the Next Question***

  The path to all answers.

- ***Be On Go***

  Don't procrastinate.

- ***Your Fate Is Inextricably Bound to the Group to Which You Belong***

  Are you "at cause" over your group or "at affect" to it?

- ***Imagination***

  The doors to the kingdom of your mind.

- ***Dreams Don't Have Expiration Dates***

  It's never too late to rehabilitate your dreams.

- ***Do as I Do***

  Follow me by doing as I do, not as I say.

- ***Claiming for Oneself***

  When your work ethic has created the highest level of certainty.

- ***Humor, Charm and Irony***

  The three components that will keep you in the room.

- ***Life Force***

  The willingness to see, be seen, and therefore, perceive.

- ***Find the Good and Praise It***

  Build strength where strength exists.

- ***The Word "No" Has to Be a Motivator***

  The word "no" must strengthen, not weaken.

- ***Your Career Is a Marathon, Not a Sprint***

  Greatness is a process that takes time—a sustained effort.

- ***Do Your Best and Forget the Rest***

  Aim for excellence, not perfection. And let the rest go until the next time.

- ***The Wrong Way Is the Right Way***

  Just start. Sir Isaac Newton said that bodies in motion tend to stay in motion. Even if you're going the wrong way, you can course correct if you're in motion.

- ***Don't Let Your Expectations Get Higher Than Your Gratitude***

  Be grateful for even the smallest thing. Don't let your ego ruin it.

- ***Your Career Should Be Déjà Vu***

  You should be able to see your postulates twice: once when you envision them and again when they become reality.

- ***Communication Is the Solvent for Everything***

  The only way to come to an agreement with everything.

- ***K-SHIT FM***

  The negative self-talk in your head is always the first to speak.

- ***K-ART FM***

  The positive affirmations created to counteract the negative self-talk.

Note: Now that you know my precepts, you'll see them ***in bold italics*** throughout the book.

Also, you'll notice I make extensive use of definitions. The dictionary has always been one of the most powerful tools for clarification and understanding of the language that people share, especially in art. Every creative person has their own language that they've learned or created. The dictionary is the one source that centralizes all understanding of what words mean and the possibilities for interpretation. Basically, it simplifies communication.

The Two Prisms

My approach to teaching is divided into two components *(separate elements of something larger)*: "Show" and "Business." These components are based on the concept of light passing through a dispersive prism.

What is a dispersive prism? It's a device that receives a singular light and breaks it up into a rainbow or myriad *(a great number)* of colors. The most common type of dispersive prism is a triangular prism.

I believe you and your energy are like a light beam entering this **Space Where Art Can Occur**. Your energy, **Life Force**, hopes and dreams are channeled or refracted through this education, methodology (procedure) and approach, thus separating that beam of light and causing a myriad of colors to emerge. These colors represent an expansion of possibilities that you may not be aware of, were hesitant to embrace or laid dormant. I want to find the best you available, and help get you beyond your limiting aspects of self. The refraction of your light into limitless, bold colors is the basis of my studio, and I use two different educational prisms to achieve this.

The first triangular prism consists of Passion, Application and Strategy. You enter into the foundational aspects of the studio, and everything going forward stands on this bedrock. This primary prism is what we are covering in this book.

The second triangular prism consists of Politics, Personality and Craft. While the first prism teaches you how to be an accomplished artist or professional, the second teaches you how to monetize your art, become a businessperson and turn it into commerce. While we won't discuss the second prism in this book, it's equally critical to your success as an artist or professional. Hence, the 360 degrees of Show Business.

The best way to put the concept of a prism into context is to compare a student entering Harvard or Howard as a freshman, (that beam of light), and going through the four to six years of education, experience, socialization and challenges associated with dream fulfillment, growth and maturity. At the end of their time there, they have changed significantly, (myriad colors have emerged), and are prepared to go out into the world and start building the life they desire.

The First Prism

Let's examine the three sides of the first prism and their corresponding components:

Passion:

- *Passion Fuels Progress.*
- *You Can't Teach Through a Frown.*
- The ability to overcome disappointment, be resilient and *Make It Go Right.*
- *There Are No Losses, Only Lessons.*
- *Your Career is a Marathon, Not a Sprint.*
- A person attached to a tangible DOIN (Declaration of Independence, aka business plan; see page 263 for details) will have a greater reason to be joyful about the journey.

Application:

- Complete knowledge and ability to manage all of the components of acting (event, behavior, the moment before, etc.)
- Mastery of the exercises (improvisation, cold readings, cold stand-up (comedy), laugh/cry/laugh, etc.)
- Ability to articulate and execute the three stages of acting development:
  - o 1. Foundation: Learning the fundamental aspects of the tools of acting.
  - o 2. Implementation: Taking that acquired skill set into the professional arena and booking jobs.
  - o 3. Execution: Actualizing your dream (Plan A) and becoming a solid working actor (Plan B).

- Understanding and mastering your "waves of casting":
  - 1st wave of casting (roles closest to your authentic self)
  - 2nd wave of casting (roles that are a bit of a stretch)
  - 3rd wave of casting (roles you have to create from the outside in)

Strategy:

- Your **Career Bus**, and how you handle the people and things that directly and indirectly influence your life and career: Parents, grandparents, significant others, siblings, agents, managers, gender, ethnicity, mortgage, pets, religion, etc. (See page 281 for details).
- Your **Relationship Map** is developed and functioning, so you're clear about what each person's relationship is to you. This includes all the people you know—friends, colleagues, employers, etc.
- You target personal and professional projects.
- Your Plan A is clear (Plan A = focus on what you can create and control)
- Your Plan B supports Plan A (Plan B = the jobs the industry has to offer)
- Your acting reel is finished and impressive.
- You've assembled your team (agent and/or manager), and the relationships are well-managed.
- You are a well-paid, working actor.

When you realize the components of the first prism, you will experience a greater understanding of yourself and who you are in relation to your acting goals and Show Business. Your dreams will be far more real and doable for you once you understand that your talent and the speed you develop are directly associated with a great passion and impeccable work ethic. As you pass through the three sides of this first prism—the acting components, the exercise components and all the foundational mindset and strategic skills—you will become a more able, inspired and fully realized artist capable of achieving your dream.

Call to Action:

At the end of each chapter, there is a call to action to encourage you to learn by participating in suggested tasks. It's an invitation to actively explore the concepts of passion, application and strategy.

The call to action is also meant to challenge and encourage you to consider how to recognize your strengths, improve on your shortcomings and handle or confront the people, places and things that stop you from achieving the career and life you envision.

Get a pad and pen to take notes. Create a journal. It will serve you as you record your observations over time.

The First Prism:
Passion

Your Passion Fuels Your Progress

Your approach affects your ability to achieve what you want. A great sense of passion will allow you to see and have more. You'll have endless opportunities throughout your journey. You will be in solution mode, fueling your life and career.

Your passion determines how you handle challenges and setbacks, whether you see them as growth opportunities or obstacles to avoid. A positive attitude will attract upbeat, like-minded people who will support and uplift you. With an optimistic outlook, you will approach every situation with enthusiasm and determination, and you will find ways to overcome the challenges that come your way.

Passion is not something that can be easily taught or learned. It is a mindset that you choose to adopt and cultivate. It requires self-awareness and a willingness to take responsibility for your thoughts and actions. You will see a significant difference in your life and career once you have developed a passionate attitude.

Passion also plays a crucial role in your creativity and **Imagination.** When you have a positive, open and passionate attitude, your mind is free to explore new ideas and think outside the box. You are not limited by self-doubt or fear; instead, you embrace curiosity and innovation. This mindset allows you to tap into your full creative potential, leading to fresh perspectives and breakthroughs in your work.

Passion impacts not only your journey, but those around you. Your energy can inspire and motivate others, creating a supportive and collaborative environment. People will be drawn to your optimism and enthusiasm, and building strong connections will be easier.

On the other hand, a dispassionate attitude will limit your potential and hinder your progress. It will repel opportunities and relationships, as people will not want to be around someone bringing negativity into their lives. A closed-off mindset will prevent you from learning and growing, and you will miss valuable lessons and experiences.

You must also understand the meaning of the precept **You Can't Teach Through a Frown.** A passionless attitude isn't inviting, and you won't let a teacher or director talk in your ear. Your distrust of the process shines through. Teaching you is impossible, so you slow down your growth and evolution. You add unnecessary years and weight to your journey.

So, remember: **Passion Fuels Progress.** Choose to approach every situation with positivity, openness and a willingness to learn and evolve. Embrace challenges as opportunities for growth and surround yourself with people who uplift and support you. With the right amount of passion, you can achieve anything you set your mind to.

A Discussion About Passion with Students

Note: Some of the most valuable lessons are learned from observing and listening to others work through their questions and curiosities. Throughout this book, I will share real conversations with my students on different topics to illuminate my core teachings.

This first discussion sets up the concept of the first prism, specifically about the "Show" of Show Business.

RICHARD

The Show component of the first prism is comprised of three foundational pillars: Passion, Application and Strategy. Passion is the most important, because everything else sits on top of that. Passion fuels progress. That is certain. That is absolute. And since 1976, when I started studying and subsequently started teaching, I have understood how absolute that is.

STUDENT 1

When you say "fuel," what does that mean?

RICHARD

If I'm teaching somebody who's open, the trajectory of that person is so much sharper and higher versus somebody who is closed off. It's hard to get through to a person who is closed off. With somebody who's open, it gets in. Passion fuels the speed at which your talent is put forth into the world. There's more hunger, interest, excitement, possibility, certainty and tangibility in your universe.

Everything is affected because it is energy. When we meet someone with positive energy, we are drawn to them. Likewise, we are put off by someone who has negative energy.

Now, some people are attracted to people with negative energy because they want what they can't have—one of the most common human traits. When you are seeking something that someone else has, be it a quality or a status in life, and you place a higher value on that than your own dream and your own vision, then you are going to be there for it, rather than it being there for you. When you're chasing your own dream or following your own purpose, albeit scary, you are more connected to it, and you have a far greater chance of manifesting what you see.

As a teacher, I can tell you that **Passion Fuels Progress**. You can take a person with lesser talent and incredible passion, and they will go further than someone with great talent who is lacking in passion. The main reason why people don't achieve their goals is because of a lack of passion. I think passion is one of the reasons I sit here today—because I've been around people who are extraordinarily passionate. I've been around some pessimistic people, hoping for optimism, but I've also been around some positive people whose optimism helped them to overcome challenges. That survivor's mentality is a product of passion.

There are great stories where 300 people overcame 10,000 people. Those people fought with ferocity because they had a purpose, and it was all in their passionate attitude. In sports, the most talented don't always win. The closest thing to death is apathy *(absence or suppression of passion, emotion or excitement)*. When you're apathetic, when you have suppressed your emotions, and you don't have anything to care about, you are just a few steps away from death—spiritually and physically. How do the rest of you relate to passion?

STUDENT 2

I really like this discussion about passion because it drives everything you do. You're going to go as far as your passion takes you because your passion affects what you do physically and mentally. It affects your actions—how you operate and your vibration level. All of that is fueled by passion. So, the actions you take because of your passion will either be good or bad. You're supposed to do the right things, and passion drives you.

RICHARD

Absolutely. I have survived over 55 years in this business. I still have as much fun as anybody else. And it's all because of my passion.

STUDENT 3

Was there a shift for you? Was there a time when your passion wasn't so great, and you made a conscious shift to change it? Or have you always had a lot of passion?

RICHARD

I have always been very passionate, except when I moved back here after I did *All My Children*, and I had not dealt with my post-traumatic stress from the plane crash. I took a two-week sabbatical, and it lasted five years. I played golf every day. I put my clubs, my friends' clubs and our suitcases in the back of my truck, and we would drive anywhere from Fresno to San Diego, from Malibu to Arizona. That's the way I dealt with my trauma until I was invited to see a scene that Milton directed from *Cat on a Hot Tin Roof* with Michelle Clunie. I wanted to get up there on that stage because her scene partner just wasn't cutting it for me. I wanted to get up on that stage and say to him, "Look, let me show you how to do this. Sit over there. Come on, Michelle. Me and you." My passion for getting on that stage and showing them how it was supposed to go woke me up and got me back into the business.

STUDENT 3

What about when you started out, before you were successful?

RICHARD

I had nothing, and when I started out, I used to hear people talking about the "struggling actor." I resented anybody even beginning to think that I was a struggling actor. Life as an aspiring actor was challenging, yes. I got kicked out of apartments. I drove totaled cars with plastic on the windows. I've slept on floors. I've slept in my truck. People took the front door off my apartment so I would have to move out. I can't even begin to tell you all the challenges, but it never stopped me. I never stopped. I was like a pitbull with lockjaw. I had a passion for my art and a belief in my talent, and I knew instinctively I wouldn't wind up where I was. I continued to pursue and pursue. I came to Los Angeles on December 4th, 1971, at 11:05 pm, and when I stepped off that plane, to this day, I have never struggled. And I've never worked another job. I came close, but I never did. And I'm still having the time of my life.

Never Let Your Creativity Pass Through the Lens of Someone Else's Morality,
Part I

Richard addresses his Scene Study class.

RICHARD

I speak to you a lot about the concept ***Never Let Your Creativity Pass Through the Lens of Someone Else's Morality.*** As you know, the basis of my teaching is ***"Do as I Do."*** I say that because I want to be an example of my own teaching. I don't want to ask you to do anything I haven't done. I have to do it to teach it. It's not "do as I say." It's ***"Do as I Do."***

Everyone here is a creator. We all have projects that we are initiating, and there are hills and valleys with those projects. I am clear about my purpose in life. It's my North Star. Sometimes, I start a new project, and it's a challenge to find my way because the purpose of this particular project is not clear to me yet. As I continue to ***Ask the Next Question***, the reason begins to reveal itself as my overall purpose adds color, dimension, logic and reasoning. Ultimately, it will evolve into something viable.

I've ***Never Allowed My Creativity To Pass Through the Lens of Someone Else's Morality***. I have stuck to my beliefs and doggedly held onto my vision even when the whole cry of voices is on the other side. And the whole cry of voices has consistently been on the other side. Regardless of that, I will not bend or give in. I give myself a chance to fail, and I insist on that. I'm sharing this because I know you all are on your own journeys. I've had many conversations recently with people challenged by the possible compromise of their dream, and they were teetering on whether they should or shouldn't allow that to happen.

Ultimately, it comes down to your sense of integrity and ethics about your vision. When you are clear about your dream and it is purpose-driven, you can see the finish line. When setting goals, most people start from where they are and look for a target somewhere in the future. On the other hand, I reverse engineer the concept of goal achievement, working backward from a desired outcome to identify the necessary steps to reach it. It's like constructing a roadmap in reverse. The first thing you plug into your GPS is your destination. Then, it tells you how to get there.

I encourage you to be clear about your dream. When you're not clear and purpose-driven, it's easy for someone to change your destination. If you have GPS, you may get re-routed, but you'll always stay on course to arrive at your destination.

Art can change the world quicker than anything. And if you want something, you have to vibrate on the same level as the thing you want. When you do, you fall in love. That's when people get scared. People are afraid to feel that. It takes three seconds to fall in love—the rest is denial. I teach people to fall in love and not deny it. To continue vibrating on that same level. When something doesn't vibrate on the same level, it is discordant. Toxic.

When you're vibrating on the same level, you can accomplish anything. So when you go and talk about your project, you have to be pregnant with it. You have to have a love for the thing that you do. You can see the people who don't. And you can see those who absolutely can't live without it. Those people can change the world. Those are the kinds of people I am encouraged to teach.

I want to get you to the level where you are not afraid of your talent, take possession of what you believe in and get other people to see it. They don't have to like it. And that's okay. They just need to get out of the way. And that includes the people on your *Career Bus*. If they don't vibrate on the same level as you, it's no problem. Open the bus door and say, "I love you, but you can't ride on this bus. I'll give you a call. Take care." Close that door and keep on going. I don't give a damn if that's your mother or father or your auntie or your dead grandparents. You still love them. They just can't ruin the energy of this journey.

Never Let Your Creativity Pass Through the Lens of Someone Else's Morality
Part II

Two students have just finished a scene. One student is assessing her work and reveals that she backed off on the sexual aspects of the character because of her own considerations.

STUDENT 1

I want to keep my dancing in the scene. I'm very proud of myself for doing that because that's not something I would normally do.

RICHARD

You don't normally dance?

STUDENT 1

I do, but not in front of people. I'm like, "Am I awkward? Do I look weird? Probably." So I'm kind of self-conscious about that, but I'm very proud of myself for doing that. It felt good. I didn't feel super weird about it. Something I would tweak is the impact of the alcohol. I could have experienced that more than I did. I would tweak the ending as well. I didn't tell my scene partner that I would be all up in their personal space, but then I didn't fully commit to that choice. If I'm going to do something, I need to commit fully.

RICHARD

What is that moment?

STUDENT 1

The moment when I'm ready to have sex with the other character.

RICHARD

So, on a second take, you would go there in terms of that.

STUDENT 1

Yes.

RICHARD

Part of your experience in this was just being able to get past your own considerations.

STUDENT 1

Yes.

RICHARD

Are they your considerations? Or are they the considerations of others?

STUDENT 1

Probably a little bit of both. My upbringing and my own standards.

RICHARD

Upbringing?

STUDENT 1

Yes. So that would be others.

RICHARD

Is the church involved in this?

STUDENT 1

Oh yeah, the church is involved in that.

RICHARD

That's a big one in terms of always being a voice over our shoulders. Are you from a very religious family?

STUDENT 1

Moderately religious. Religious upbringing? Yes. Now, people are not as religious.

RICHARD

Okay. Who in your family would be the most critical of this behavior?

STUDENT 1

My godmother.

RICHARD

Your godmother?

STUDENT 1

Yes. Not my mom. My mom is very expressive. She's not as strict. She might be surprised if she saw me do a part like this, but she'd get over it.

RICHARD

Being free to explore is a big thing in art, because it's very difficult to separate who we are from what we do. And today, it's even *more* difficult because of cancel culture. People think that they're going to get ostracized for thinking, expressing or creating art in a very particular way. I have a client who's a series regular, and he's flying without a net—the stuff he's experiencing and exploring as his character can and will be the subject of a lot of people's fascination, applause or condemnation because it's in that territory.

One of the things we have to do as artists is to look at what we actually want to create in terms of our dreams. You're a beautiful, sensual and funny woman. The kind of roles people will see you in will have these areas that will ring the bell of your personal considerations. It's a question of what kind of career you want. We have that problem with women from the Middle East. If you look at what's happening right now in Iran, there's a revolution. There was a young woman who didn't properly wear the traditional garb and didn't have her hair covered up—which, by their laws, she should have. She was arrested, and she died in custody. Now, there's a revolution amongst women over there because of religious limitations.

So if this person were an artist who grew up in these cultures, they'd have a hell of a way to go trying to figure out what kind of career they want to have because they risk being ostracized. It depends on your family, your religion and all kinds of things. Using women from the Middle East is an extreme example of it, but on the shorter side of things, there's a whole list of considerations that people can have. And I think you have to take a look at this.

What you did tonight was beautiful. Very interesting, provocative and moment-to-moment. All of the things you wanted to do regarding acting, you did. You were patient. You had a relationship with the other character. You had reflective delay taking things in and showing how you felt about them. There were things you had an opinion about. And then, embarrassment and discomfort with music and dance and how you felt about the audience. I wondered about the placement of that table because it feels like you have an Ikea store between the two of you. And you have it close enough to you to make sure no quick moves of intimacy can be made in the scene. I wonder if that was by design or what. But you did a great job. Fantastic work for your first scene.

But in the bigger picture, it's what you see for yourself. I would say you're a leading lady. Thank God there are so many shows with Black characters in them compared to when I came up. There was ABC, CBS, NBC and the occasional movie. They didn't think that stories about Black people sold. They didn't believe our product would sell in Europe or the rest of the world. Well, now they know better. There's a plethora of opportunities. So it's a question of how you see yourself. What kinds of shows do you see yourself in? What parts could you take that actress out and put yourself in?

STUDENT 1

I see myself doing parts like Gabrielle Union.

RICHARD

Gabrielle is dangerous as hell.

STUDENT 1

She is! I love her.

RICHARD

But you notice that her life is set up like that, right? Her man protects her right to be that. You need to have a **Space Where Art Can Occur** so that your surroundings and the people in your world support you. Okay, Gabrielle Union. Who else?

STUDENT 1

I also like a lot of the stuff that Issa Rae did on *Insecure*. I watched *Boomerang* again over the weekend. I looked at Robin Givens' character and I said, *I want to do that*. I don't want to be afraid to be provocative and dangerous in that way. I don't want to be scared of my sexuality and those types of roles. These are things I want to do and not shy away from.

RICHARD

Right. Cool. We see what we have to handle. We also see the people we have to handle, like your godmother. You give your godmother more power than you do your own mother. What is that about? And that calls for a meeting with your godmother so that she can understand what you do and that your choices as an artist are not moral in nature. They're not limited in nature. Who you are and what you do are two different things. Do you understand me?

STUDENT 1

Absolutely.

RICHARD

We will do that. But it takes diligence and fearlessness to identify your **Career Bus** (see page 281). Have you done that?

STUDENT 1

I have.

RICHARD

Have you handled your bus?

STUDENT 1

No, because I'm scared of what my godmother would say about a role like this. So, I think I still have some handling to do.

RICHARD

Okay, I just want to do something right quick.

Richard turns to the class and asks another student to grab a chair and sit directly across from Student 1. Richard tells Student 1 to play the role of her godmother and to have a conversation about Hollywood with the newly-seated student as if she were her goddaughter. At some point, Richard stops the conversation and tells the students to switch seats. Student 1 plays herself, and Richard tells her to answer her godmother.

RICHARD

Good. Now, that was strong.

The class cheers and applauds.

STUDENT 1

I feel confident in that. I feel like I could tell my godmother that.

RICHARD

Right. So, tomorrow. Did you notice her eyes raised when I said that? Tomorrow. Handle it tomorrow. Make the phone call and say you need to talk with her face to face. Is she nearby?

The student reveals where her godmother lives.

RICHARD

Drive there. That's how important this is. It's called **Radical Remission.**

STUDENT 1

Radical Remission?

RICHARD

Radical Remission. What does that mean? Can someone tell me what that means?

STUDENT 2

It means having zero tolerance for anything that is holding you back. So you're radically going against those habits that block you. You're taking a radical stance; moving forward is the only direction.

RICHARD

Right. Because if it's cancer, you better act now. **Radical Remission** means you are acting aggressively to get it out. Because you can't operate in half-measures. According to Alcoholics Anonymous and all of the anonymous groups out there—you can't halfway stop drinking. You have to radically stop it and do whatever it takes to not go back. There are no half-measures to anything, especially when it comes to your life, your career, belief system and purpose. You have to handle stuff swiftly, like a guillotine. Immediately. You got this. I want you to handle this tomorrow. I want you to drive your ass down there. And if you need to make a phone call before you go into the house, do so. Call me. Or call any one of the teachers here. And watch the change in you.

Being a Star

Let's break this down and make the comparison between a celestial star and an artistic star.

A star is a massive, gaseous celestial body that generates light and heat through nuclear fusion.

A star artist has a large and dedicated fanbase akin to the immense size of a celestial body. An artist usually occupies a unique and elevated position in the public eye, much like a star in the sky. A star artist creates their unique style and influence, illuminating their audience and inspiring others, much like a star emitting light and heat.

In essence, just as a star is a powerful, influential force in the universe, a star artist is a luminary in their respective field, captivating and inspiring their audience with their talent and creativity.

A star is self-luminous because it is a celestial body (*something of the heavens*). It consists of a mass of gas held together by its gravity. Thus, this suggests that the mass of gas is the source of the lumens *(the total amount of visible light)* and the generator of the nuclear reactions in its interior. It does not need anything else to persist because it survives of its own volition *(done of one's own will)*. As a result, all this powerful energy going toward the surface is balanced by the inward-directed gravitational forces. To put it simply, ***Outflow Equals Inflow***.

I've experienced this understanding of a star while working with major talents on different projects. These are people who have achieved a tremendous amount of success in their careers and lives. And the one thing I find with those who have that sense of balance is that they know who they are. They live beautifully in this light that they put out. And because of their luminosity, they attract energy that supports their balance. There is a sense of peace, nourishment and enjoyment in their exchange with the universe. That sense of energy balance, also known as reaping what you sow, means that the energy you receive equals what you put out there.

There is also an incredible exchange between this source of light and the people who receive it. They are grateful for it. I have noticed people I admire have this self-luminous aspect. They understand that they are celestial in being, handle it well and enjoy the exchange. I've seen it in people like Magic Johnson. Magic puts so much into the universe with his generosity, consciousness and empathy for others, and I see it come back to him tenfold. I saw it when I worked with Burt Reynolds, one of the most generous guys in the world. I saw it with Richard Thomas when he was a big star from *The Waltons,* and we did a play together. I saw it with Steven Spielberg. I've worked with so many great people, and I can always feel the beautiful way in which they share their gifts. They are stars. And that's what being one is.

Call to Action:

Here's an opportunity to examine your passion and how open you are to receiving this new approach to becoming a consummate artist. I challenge you to step outside your comfort zone and consider a 360-degree approach to mastering Show Business. Change is on the other side of discomfort.

Take a look at your communication skills:

- Are you a good listener?
- Do you acknowledge what you heard and repeat it back to confirm?
- Do you empathize?
- Do you always have to be right?
- Do you operate through blame, shame and regret?
- Do you try to resolve disagreements?
- Are your opinions and ideas influenced by what others think?
- Do you bring light to the rooms you enter?
- Are you more of an optimist or pessimist?

Write down your answers to these questions. Notice where strength exists and where you can build it. How can you increase your star power?

The First Prism: Application

The Acting Lexicon
(The Language of Acting)

I have been an actor since March 7, 1969, when I realized that acting is what I was put on this earth to do. That day, I became very clear about my purpose, which has never changed.

I've been on vacation for 55 years and counting. I love being an artist. I live to create. Nothing makes me happier than to originate something and, by **Asking the Next Question**, bring it to fruition.

Over the years, I have been curious about the teachings and philosophy of masters like Konstantin Stanislavski, Herbert Berghof, Sanford Meisner, Michael Shurtleff, Lee Strasberg and Elia Kazan. Each had a respectable and impressive list of actors and artists they helped develop. I studied with two masters myself: Stella Adler and Milton Katselas. After Lee Strasberg died, Milton was arguably considered the preeminent acting teacher in the world.

Milton studied with Kazan, Joshua Logan and Strasberg, took the best of their techniques, and devised his own acting methodology. It is an approach drawn from many disciplines of life outside of tried and true acting nomenclatures and processes, including religious traditions, spiritual philosophies, pool room protocols and plain old common sense. Milton realized that one size doesn't fit all. Each student or actor had their own sensibility, background and experience that resonated differently from the same information, input or circumstance. The concept of a technique seemed limiting and fixed. He had an innate ability to know the exact elixir *(a magical or medicinal concoction)* that would draw out of the actor their best and unique selves.

Milton's mastery initially influenced my approach to teaching. Much of what he taught me informed the foundation of a consistent career as a working actor, which has flourished over five decades. While Milton inspired my purview, the dual track of acting and teaching showed me how to be a good actor and have a successful career. I have taken what Milton taught me, expanded upon it and taken it to the next level.

In the following pages, I will share some of the application modalities *(method, procedure and process)* and tools that are necessary to understand how to build a character, how to play the part, how to understand what the writer is asking of you and ultimately, how to breathe life into this human being you are portraying. The language is fairly universal, so there should be little confusion about what we're discussing. However, I have added some elements that, for most, will be a new approach to studying the structure of art that I deem necessary to achieve the highest degree of character and story development. I'm bringing science into the equation of creation.

I read somewhere about the importance of art in relation to STEM, (Science, Technology, Engineering and Math), and that the creativity that STEM people possess is often motivated and inspired by the artistic side of their brains. Adding art brings personal expression into the hard sciences.

While some may see art and science as being on opposite ends of the spectrum, they have much more to offer each other than you might think. The left brain versus right brain dominance theory suggests that the right hemisphere is more involved in creative tasks, such as recognizing faces and interpreting emotions, which could be associated with artistic abilities. The left hemisphere is often linked with analytical tasks, such as language processing and logical reasoning.

Art is an effective means of expressing and communicating the sciences. Likewise, the problem-solving abilities of a mathematician or scientist can benefit an artist. As you will notice, a lot of my teaching reaches into the areas of STEM. This is because, as I continued to study and understand structure and its necessity, I realized that being an artist is a science.

According to Oxford Languages, the definition of science is "the systematic study of the structure and behavior of the physical and natural world through observation and experimentation."[1]

As actors, we are studying the nature of human beings. We are behavioral scientists.

I also looked up the definition of anthropology. According to the National Park Service, anthropology is the scientific study of humans and their cultural, social, biological and environmental aspects of life in the past and the present.[2] I realized that, as actors, that's exactly what we do.

In art, part of the anthropology of a subject or a character has to do with tendencies. You must understand that person's cultural, behavioral, emotional, physical and spiritual aspects. When you study those aspects, you get to know their nature, and you grow to expect certain things from that person's tendencies.

You become a behavioral anthropologist who uses the scientific approach of systematic study to discover who this person is, what they think and why they react in a certain way.

Having more access to those colors allows you to be more creative and gives you more options in creating a character.

Event (Obvious and Real)

The definition of 'event' from Dictionary.com: "An occurrence, especially one of some importance."[3]

The first question to ask when you are trying to build a character and find an understanding of a particular scene is "what is it about?"

Here's an example:

The scene is a wedding. Your character, Meredith, is the bride. She is very nervous, as most newlyweds are. She's marrying an identical twin, Calvin. There is a lot of drama surrounding the wedding because Calvin's twin brother, Alvin, moved away a year earlier and hasn't shown up as expected—he was supposed to be the best man. Unbeknownst to everyone, Meredith was secretly involved with Alvin before establishing a relationship with Calvin. The wedding is proceeding without Alvin.

As you start asking questions to understand the event of a scene, remember that there are always two components to consider when talking about an event: the obvious event and the real event.

The obvious event is on the surface. It's what the writer gives you. It is tied to the words in the script. It's the outward action in the scene.

The real event is associated with the character's subtext (unspoken thoughts). The inner life of the character is what is really happening.

The wedding is the obvious event. The character has to fulfill all the requirements to make this event as full and vibrant as possible. In this instance, Meredith has to go against the undercurrent of the impending trouble. The end of the scene has to be somewhat present in the beginning by virtue of her behavior: Seemingly extraordinarily happy, yet on the verge of tears. The character takes care of everyone else but neglects her own preparation and needs. How heavily is this secret weighing on her at this point?

The family prepares the venue and makes a fuss about the reality of this auspicious occasion. Finally, it's time for the ceremony.

So far, this obvious event—(the wedding and all the energy surrounding it)—is tied to what the writer is giving you. The excitement is palpable.

The real event is connected to the stuff that is unspoken but strongly felt. For example, the maid of honor discovers Meredith in the bathroom, bawling her eyes out while she's reading a text.

Some questions the actor preparing to play Meredith's character might be interested in include: Who sent the text? Could it possibly have come from Alvin? If Alvin and Meredith's secret were to be revealed, could it destroy the intended outcome of the marriage? Will she bring shame and destruction upon herself and all the loved ones attending? Is she making a mistake by going forward? Does she love Alvin more?

The real event is about the things not necessarily on the surface or in the dialogue itself. It doesn't necessarily reveal itself in overt communication. It's the stuff connected to the subtext that lies below the surface of the obvious. So ask yourself: *What's really going on?*

Call to Action:

As you go through your day, observe the exchanges you have with others, and their exchanges with other people. Pay attention to what is said and what is not, and write it all down in your journal.

To What Degree/Extent?

Once you determine the real event of a scene, you must ask questions to evaluate it. Determining the level of evaluation, or "to what degree," helps you calculate your emotional experience/response. This empowers you to under-stand the degree of importance of an event and how to play it.

The degree of the emotional response and the degree to which the real event reveals itself will be determined by where you are in the story. You will emotionally respond to an event differently on page one versus how you respond to an event on page 80.

When a scene is in the first act of the movie or the play, you must understand that the writer is setting things up—for example, someone embarking on a hero's journey. When we get to the second act, things fall apart until the character hits rock bottom, becomes a warrior and fights back. That hero carries themself into the third act where they ultimately become a martyr. To appraise this emotional ride and arc of the character entails determining to what degree something is being experienced.

In other words, you have to assess the entire artistic experience. If you put the script's first act on a scale from one to ten in emotional intensity, the first act is probably one to four. Then, the first half of the second act is five to six until the main character hits bottom. And then, when the character starts to fight back as a warrior in the second half of the second act, the evaluation rises to seven, eight, nine or even a ten. Finally, it levels off during the martyr stage of the third act.

You constantly have to determine where you are in the process of communicating a significant event. Determine the intensity, degree, and level to which something is being experienced.

Call to Action:

When observing others communicate, note the degree of intensity as they engage. Notice whether the conversation intensifies as it goes on. To understand the levels, evaluate the degrees of emotion on a scale of 1-10. Now, describe the exchange you observed in your journal, including the levels.

The Moment Before

The most critical moment in a scene is the moment before. It contains all the data that allows you to start a scene with the appropriate amount of energy, emotion, history and intention. The moment before sets the tone and trajectory of the scene. The reality of the moment before can only be determined by the event of the scene. When you know what the scene is about, you can shape a clear moment before that supports the event and helps you start the scene.

The moment before dictates your behavior and physical/emotional state. It fuels your character's life and experience before the scene begins. You should feel a life in progress when you enter the stage or the camera's frame in a movie. You should already be in belief with the event of the scene as you enter.

However, most actors don't do that. They start the scene on the first line. There isn't that initial "plié" into the scene. A plié means to bend, and is a term used in ballet. A dancer will bend at the knee to spring forward into a dance move. The plié sets up everything, and evaluating it influences everything afterward. There is a life and experience that needs to be examined before the first line of the scene is spoken. That background will offer you the plié into the scene.

Let's go back to the event of the wedding. For Meredith's character to be fully realized, we must understand her history with Calvin and his family, especially with his brother. If they are identical twins, there are striking similarities between the two. That history has to be created. Meredith's history with the family has to be created. The expectations of both families, hers

59

and his, have to be devised and understood. The doubters and supporters must be delineated. All of this will affect her on this day.

Generally speaking, marriages are totally about what happened before, because that affects the behavior on this day. An actor has to be filled with that specific emotional history and information before they start the scene.

These previous elements will affect Meredith's behavior while reading the text in the bathroom. Her emotional, physical and spiritual history will influence what she says and how she reacts.

If you don't leave the train station with the right amount of fuel and people to run the train—the conductor, engineer, servers and porters—you will not have a successful trip. Similarly, if you don't have the proper information to fuel yourself, you cannot play the character and the scene because you don't have the necessary impetus, energy and reasoning. If you don't understand the event, you can't start your train going down the right track. Proper attention needs to be paid to the moment before. It gives you that specific plié into the life and experience of a character and event.

Call to Action:

As you observe people enter a room, note what they could be thinking and feeling. What's your first impression? Briefly describe what you see on the surface in your journal, then get into the emotional subtext of the "characters" in your scene.

Behavior

Behavior is an underestimated acting tool. In my school, we teach you to be a specific person in a specific place having a specific experience, and we utilize behavior in your acting work to achieve that.

Let's look at what Dictionary.com says about behavior: "Manner of behaving or acting; that observable activity in a human or animal; the aggregate of responses to internal and external stimuli."[4] (I love that one).

Also: A stereotyped, species-specific activity, such as a courtship dance or startle reflex; the action or reaction of any material under given circumstances.

You can tell a lot about people by their behavior. For example, imagine standing across the street from a person sitting at a bus stop. Their movements and expressions will undoubtedly reveal a ton of information about their life.

Look closely, and you might notice their foot tapping uncontrollably. That shaking foot reveals the energy and nervous activity of what's happening inside that person. What possible event in their mind is making them behave in this manner?

Or perhaps the person you're observing is hunched over, wringing their hands and sighing from time to time. What could be causing this particular behavior? Are they overworked and underpaid? Underappreciated by their boss or colleagues? Are they struggling to make ends meet this month?

Maybe the person at the bus stop is having an animated discussion with someone else. Depending on their behavior, you can tell if this is a new relationship, an established, comfortable relationship or a relationship that is two seconds away from breaking up. Each of these relationships represents different events that affect the couple's behavior.

Behavior is an essential part of learning about the components of acting. It's a critical aspect of character building to understand and reveal certain aspects of this individual's life— what they think and what's going on. It indicates the character's inner life. Behavior is also how one physically lives and operates in a particular environment under a specific event (*the aggregate of responses to internal and external stimuli*).

Let's go back to the wedding. Meredith's behavior is influenced by this event, (especially this secret she's withholding), and all that comes with it: the environment, the other characters, her inner life and the moment before. Given the external and internal stimuli, how does she physically behave and operate in the scene? Her actions and expressions will give a sense of where she is mentally, emotionally and physically in relation to the event. Some possible behaviors that Meredith could be experiencing as a result of this event include bawling, pacing uncontrollably, sweating, almost passing out, feeling nauseous, etc.

The other half of understanding behavior is that the process of behaving in a theatrical production and on film are very, very different. You must act according to the stage you are working on.

Let's look at the stage first. If you're working in a 100-seat black box theater, the life you create as a character in a play must resonate with the people sitting in the back row. You need to be seen, heard and felt. Working in that size of theater requires specific, intentional communication. Your behavior must be large enough to translate and express the inner and outer life of the character.

If you're working at the Shubert Theater in New York City, which has 1,502 seats, being seen, heard and felt from the back row requires much more energy, voice, intention and emotion to create an inner and outer life that delivers the message. Everything is a little larger in expression.

Conversely, in film, where the camera and mics surround you and can pick up the subtlest expression and movement, the director may instruct you to reduce your behavior to almost imperceptible levels.

Remember this: Stage is about what you say. Film is about what you don't say.

What you don't say is called subtext. Subtext is everything in film. The subtext on stage is translated more through physical behavior. For instance, if a character is impinged *(deeply affected)* by something on film, the subtext is in the character's eyes. On stage, it's communicated by a physical reaction or gesture.

Depending on the director, you may do the same scene 20, 50, 60 or 70 times in a film to complete the setup. There are well-documented stories of 15-20 takes or more to capture just one angle. Depending on the number of actors, a scene will have several setups to complete.

It starts with a wide master shot. Then, a tighter master, which you may have to do several takes to get right. Move in for a two-shot if there are two people in the scene. Maybe a moving camera shot. An over-the-shoulder shot. A tighter over. A dirty over. A close-up. A tighter close-up. Then, the director will have you do the same thing from the other side.

What I just described could be 50 different takes from all angles. People rely on their memory to access emotions. And sometimes, the memory does work to elicit emotions. But it doesn't sustain most people—particularly through 50-60 takes of the same scene.

This is where muscle memory kicks in. Muscle memory is connected to behavior and emotion. When you call upon muscle memory connected to specific moments in your life, you can repeatedly duplicate that behavior and the emotion it elicits.

For example, if you see someone get hit by a car, your emotional response may trigger a physical reaction where you raise your hands to cover your face as you exclaim, "Ohhhh noooo!" By the same token, if you cover your face exactly as you did on the day and with the same level of expression of "Ohhhh noooo!" and diving into the same position of belief, that physical manifestation can trigger your memory and activate the same feelings as when you saw the initial accident. Our bodies store these memories in our muscles, and will activate accordingly.

Call to Action:

Think about an event in your life, like a funeral, wedding or interview, and see if you can recall your behavior. Were you nervous? If so, was your hand shaking? Were you short of breath or having difficulty focusing? Did your voice quiver when you spoke? Were you sweating? Remember all the details of what you experienced and how you behaved, and write it in your journal.

Be Your Best Self

A common note from my acting teachers is to be a specific person in a specific place having a specific experience. From situational comedies to fantasy/sci-fi shows to procedurals and sketch variety shows, the one thing that draws us in is, "Is this person believable and relatable, no matter how highly evaluated the scene is?"

For example, if you are looking at a farce, ask yourself, "Is that an ordinary person in an extraordinary circumstance?" This is fundamental to capturing your audience's attention— entertaining or engaging realistically.

This is where all the cold exercises, which we talk about later in this book, prove invaluable. The cold exercises are essential to bringing a natural reality to your work. When you do a lot of exercises where you can't be premeditated and can only rely on your impulses, perceptions and instincts, you learn pretty quickly that you are enough. And the more centered and present you are, the more you can use your **Imagination** and sensibilities to impinge and be impinged. You will be able to work from the inside out or the outside in, if that's what presents itself at the moment. You learn to trust yourself.

The other important thing is to bring all of you, including your ethnicity, language and accent. You are offering what is true for you, thereby calling upon something you don't have to think about. It's second nature, or in this case, first nature. You are not trying to be something else to fit in.

Actors get into trouble when they try to be derivative *(unoriginal)*.

To be a person is to be your best, unfiltered self.

Call to Action:

As you go about your day, observe the people you encounter during your journey. Notice the clerk at the checkout counter, the Uber driver or the person working at the gas and electric company. All these people have very specific attitudes, personalities, behavior, dress and routines to carry out their jobs.

Record your observations in your journal, and as you do, consider what makes them so specific to their worlds. You know the drill—be descriptive and detailed.

Inner and Outer Life

Subtext and inner and outer life are kissing cousins. They are so closely related that one could *almost* be defined as the other. The difference is that subtext is more about what's being withheld— what they're *thinking*. The inner life is what the character is *feeling*.

Throughout most of the day, all of us have some form of inner and outer life. We think and feel things based on our experiences with people, places and things. For example, I am claustrophobic for several reasons. When I was probably six years old, I crawled underneath my sister's bed, and there was a lot of dust on the floor. My sister, who was a big woman, jumped on the bed. Because it was a cheap mattress, the bottom of the springs came down. She was sitting on top of me, and the springs held me in place. I couldn't move. As I gasped for air, I started choking on the dust underneath the bed. I screamed because I was scared to death.

There were deep thoughts of me dying at the age of six because of this tight space. I had shortness of breath. My heart was beating through the roof. I was screaming. I was panicking. My hands and my body were vibrating. I felt like I was going to stop breathing altogether. That was my first behavioral experience being claustrophobic. Now, anytime I'm in a situation where it's dusty, tightly enclosed or otherwise suffocating, those feelings activate in me. All of this is based on and activated by muscle memory. The muscle memory is that inner life.

So, for example, if I'm talking to someone in an elevator, and the elevator suddenly stops working, the muscle memory of the claustrophobia I experienced at age 6 starts to kick in. And as I'm standing there with that person, I don't want them to know that. This memory activates my inner life, and my outer life is trying to be present. That feeling inside affects my outer life, and it may push me to talk faster, move around the elevator, start pushing buttons or text a friend. It becomes a behavioral thing. What's happening on the outside differs from what's happening on the inside.

That is inner and outer life. The inner life is driven by feelings and muscle memory. The outer life is the behavior trying to cover for or manage what's going on in the inner life. In drama, "inner life" and "outer life" refer to different aspects of a character's existence. The two are intertwined. The external action is motivated by what the character carries inside and informs the texture of the dialogue. A character's outer life is often a reflection or manifestation of their inner life. This dynamic interplay between a character's inner and outer life adds depth and realism to their portrayal in drama.

Call to Action:

As you observe people engaging with each other—especially in a high-stakes situation like a fight—pay particular attention to what is being said and what is not being said. Afterward, write detailed notes about the scene in your journal, and see if you can discern what is underneath (inner life) by the way it comes out (outer life).

Humor

Humor is a vital part of any communication and storytelling. It is a tool that can bring levity, clarity and a deeper understanding of a project. In some of the greatest and darkest projects ever made, humor was a crucial part of the communication of that script, story, idea, film or play.

Earlier, we talked about the scene's event. When you discover the event of a scene, go the other way. Utilize **Humor, Charm and Irony**. Because if you go right down into the heart of the problem—if you play the problem right away—we already know the conclusion. So why look at it? Why stay interested as an audience? As an actor, you always have to find the opposite. You don't want to be on the nose. In storytelling, you have to preserve the moment of revelation at the end. This way, the audience doesn't know the entire story. They don't see the end in the beginning. They might sense it, but the action keeps them guessing.

It is important for you to find and develop your own unique sense of humor. All comedy is not for everyone. You can take the funniest comedians in the world and give them their own sitcom, and they're not as funny. They are funnier in their standup show because their standup is unabridged (*unfiltered and authentic*). They don't have to conform to ratings standards. You, as an artist, must cultivate your own sense of humor. You have to find the gold in it. And you have to find it within the genre that you're comfortable with.

As a teacher, I create spontaneous exercises where people can't predetermine or pre-think what's funny. Instead, it must be discovered in the moment. If you are present and interested, as opposed to trying to be interesting—which is trying to be funny—then your humor will come out. You're not thinking about it, and you're not trying to prove anything. Instead, you're being spontaneous and dealing with the reality of what's in front of you. An unexpected invitation to do a cold stand-up, song, dance or improvisation brings out a person's natural qualities. Humor is vital for an artist to be their best selves and express their unique point of view.

Call to Action:

On a day-to-day basis, track the things that you find humor in. What is funny to you? If you have an impulse to share something you find amusing, take the risk and say it. Have the courage. You are more humorous than you think.

Later, take notes in your journal about what cracks you up and what you said or did to make others laugh.

Moment-to-Moment

You can only live moment-to-moment because you don't know what's happening next. When you go to the grocery store, you don't know who you will run into. You don't know what someone's going to say to you. You don't know if you're gonna slip on a spill in aisle 12. You may know what you want to buy at the store, but then you come across something irresistible like Rice Krispies Treats. And you say to yourself, "I need that." But you know you shouldn't, so you put it back on the shelf. If you're like me, maybe you grab it again. You deal with it one moment at a time. Sugar addicts understand what I'm saying because when you are addicted to something, you sometimes don't know what the outcome will be. But you do it anyway.

Living moment-to-moment is about having the ability to deal with whatever's in front of you. Some actors think that moment-to-moment is, "Let me just be still and not do anything. And let me not be too high or too low. And I'm just going to wait for whatever comes to me, and then I'll deal with it."

Okay, but in relation to creating a particular character, which you've been hired to do, the way to get to a real moment-to-moment experience is not an exercise in you being you. It is an exercise in utilizing your knowledge as a behavioral anthropologist who uses the scientific approach of systematic study to find out who this person is, what they think and why they react in a certain way.

After you have completed all of your research and discoveries of the character and have a thorough and confident point of view, take your character out in public. Do the work, and then arrive at a place where you can forget about it because it is now in the marrow of your bones, and therefore, you can be present. Now, you can truly live moment-to-moment as a specific person in a specific place, having a specific experience that embodies all your work.

Moment-to-moment also includes being a good listener so that you can be affected by the information, acknowledge it and respond accordingly. Make sure that the person you're interacting with receives your response and is also affected by it. Being a good listener means that the work operates from the standpoint of, "I cannot hit a tennis ball until it arrives." How it arrives dictates how I hit it back—whether I lob it or take a backhand down the line. I can only make that decision after I receive the ball.

Call to Action:

A key to understanding moment-to-moment is the ability to listen, be impinged by the exchange, and respond accordingly to what you received. In your exchange with others, try having a little more patience and see if your interactions are more fruitful.

Now, journal about an exchange you've had with someone when you're fully present and engaged. What do you observe about your reactions? And what did you notice about their response?

Mother's Gold Cross

Sometimes, objects can be a great source of emotional, psychological, physical and spiritual motivation. When my mother was buried in the Catholic Church, they gave me a cross of Jesus Christ as a memento. It meant a lot to me. I would see that cross and I would get emotional. I wouldn't necessarily break down and sob—that was also possible—but sometimes, the cross would bring a tear to my eye because I would have remembered my mom and her life of labor. She chose to work hard, and she cared for her family. One of the ways she showed her love was to leave behind more than she received. So, she worked 16 hours a day. For 16 years, she worked that hard. And so that cross meant a lot to me.

I remember doing a scene in a play that called for a deep emotional connection. There was a meeting with another character at a desk, and I put my mother's cross in one of the desk drawers. During the conversation with the other character, I would open the drawer and hold the cross in my hand. Sometimes, I would stop for a minute and look at the cross as if I were pausing to think about what I wanted to say next. Touching that cross became a source of emotion for me because I allowed its energy to affect me and my response to my scene partner.

Personal objects can have a tremendous effect on a particular moment. The way you respond is the way that object makes you feel. It can give you moments of joy, laughter and deep pain. You can feed off of its energy. It's essential to understand the option of using physical objects to enhance the interpretation of a role or a character.

For example, in the film *Wall Street*, Gordon Gekko (Michael Douglas) takes advantage of his protégé, Bud Fox (Charlie Sheen), and puts him in a no-win situation. Bud goes to Gordon's office to confront him. He really wants to kill him, but the writer doesn't provide that in his writing. However, that threat should be present in the scene.

So, if I were coaching Charlie Sheen, I might tell him to put a fake gun in his pocket. That object could provide the subtextual motivation necessary to drive the scene and take it to another level.

Call to Action:

Find something extremely personal to you: a locket, letter, ring or photo. Carry it with you during your daily travels, and pull it out from time to time while you're engaging with others.

In your journal, describe how you feel when you touch that meaningful object, and record examples of how it helps change the energy in the room when you use it as a touchstone.

God is in the Details

When you observe a character's portrayal on stage, film or television, the absence of details is the first thing that can make the character less believable.

For instance, you read a script, and the script says that the character has a southern accent. Well, there is no such thing as a "southern accent." Accents and dialects vary from place to place. If you're playing a character from Louisiana, that's still too general. You have to be more specific. Where in Louisiana is your character from? Are they from Lafayette, which is Cajun? Cajuns talk with a sing-song quality to their voice. Or are they from New Orleans, which is Creole? New Orleans has a specific sound, mostly because there is a direct influence from France—more sophisticated and upper class.

If you do the necessary research about the character's accent, you will be better able to understand their background and influences. *Ask the Next Question* to reach that level of detail.

Sometimes, the writer will describe the characters as drunk. Well, drunk has to be specific. How drunk are they? What kind of drunk are they? Are they a happy drunk or a sad drunk? What are they drinking? Beer? Tequila? Bourbon? How many drinks have they had? One, two, three, four drinks? Why are they drinking? Are they an alcoholic? Are they allergic to alcohol? They're the nicest person in the world, but when they drink, do they turn into the opposite? Keep *Asking the Next Question* to create exact details about this character's physical state.

These are all examples of elements that create specificity of character. How many times have you seen a person holding a cigarette in their hand and puffing on it, pretending to smoke? Anyone who has ever been a smoker knows that person has never smoked a cigarette in their life. It takes the viewer out of the film. Sometimes, the right shoes or clothes illuminate a character because of these precise details. Does the character have a very particular limp? Do they have a bad ankle, knee or hip? Is one leg shorter than the other?

Details help the actor make the character believable, thus making the story more engaging and absorbing.

Call to Action:

When you watch a film or TV show, look for when the story tracks logically and nothing happens to make you question anything, versus the stories that don't track logically, and you catch things that are distracting or don't make sense.

As we've been discussing, precise details make all the difference. So, take notes in your journal when an actor does something that seems inauthentic to a character. Is their accent off? Do they puff on a cigar in a strange way, making it clear they've never smoked a cigar before?

Objectives

Objective:
1. Something that you strongly seek out.

Children learn objectives at a very young age. When they have their minds set on something they have to have, kids can be very clever about how they get it.

When my daughter reached driving age, her ability to attain something reached a black belt skill level. Here's an example of a conversation I had with her when I was in the kitchen one day, washing dishes:

DAUGHTER

Hey, Dad, you want some help?

Richard's daughter makes small talk, something about the news or what's going on at school. Richard looks at her sideways because he can tell something is up.

RICHARD

Okay, what is it that you really want?

DAUGHTER

I just saw you washing the dishes, and I wanted to give you a hand.

RICHARD

Man, come on. What do I look like? Booboo the Clown? Tell me what you want.

DAUGHTER

Okay. Are you using the car tonight?

RICHARD

So, you want to borrow the car?

DAUGHTER

Yes.

RICHARD

So, why didn't you just ask me?

DAUGHTER

Well, I know how you are about your car. And, okay, I should have just come out and asked you, but can I use the car?

Now, it was clear what she was seeking. But her approach was deflective, and she tried to go around the back door to get it. Evidently, there was a time element involved because she was talking fast and speeding through the chore. Those dishes were clanging into the drying rack.

Objectives are related to a larger goal. In this case, my daughter needed to get somewhere quickly. When you apply the element of the real event (her purpose in coming to me) and the element of to what degree (the urgency in which she needed the car) to an objective (her getting a yes to drive it), that objective will drive the scene.

Call to Action:

Church is a great place to observe when someone has an objective and whether they are successful in accomplishing it. Every Sunday, the preacher's sermon has an objective they are trying to fulfill. Observe how successfully they reached that goal and what was missing if they didn't, and write your impressions down in your journal. And if you don't attend church, you can do the same kind of exercise when viewing any motivational speaker.

Unpredictable Choices

All art forms require structure. For writers, the story must have a beginning, middle and end. The character must also be well structured. To portray a character, you must realize your purpose within the overall story and then fulfill that purpose, as the writer has suggested. And sometimes, that structure can become a blueprint of the story's ebbs and flows that show you where the right and left turns are, along with the ups and downs.

If you as an artist are not skillful, your actions and choices can become very predictable, making the work less interesting. When this happens, the audience tunes out. Have you ever watched something and said the line before the actor said it? You get what I'm saying.

The unexpected choices actors make in telling a structured story express unpredictability, based on a random decision or personal whim. Unpredictable choices give your work an improvisational feel and keep the audience off-balance. They don't know what's really happening or will happen.

By taking an unexpected route, you contradict what seems to be the reason or system laid out by the writer. Thus, unpredictable choices keep the viewers invested and trying to guess which way it's going to go: who's the guilty one, whose fault it is, who's the betrayer and whether the relationship is going to overcome its trials and tribulations.

Some actors have become famous based on their skill in making unpredictable or random choices. Think Marlon Brando in *The Godfather*. Francis Ford Coppola famously found a cat wandering around the set and wordlessly handed it to Brando.

Brando could've done anything with the feline, but he chose to lovingly pet it while making a deal with a desperate man. That unexpected choice instantly made the character of Don Corleone at once complex and menacing and created an iconic cinematic moment.

So, the question may arise, "How does one arrive at an unpredictable choice?" First, learn to sing the song as written. Do what the writer intended and do that well. Once you do that, you will know how to go against the grain of the song in a way that doesn't tear down its structure or rewrite the story. You must go with the structure of what the writer has given you first, before you can go against it. Otherwise, you are writing your own story.

If you do the work to understand a given story, you can make unpredictable choices. By doing all the work, your choices will enhance and reveal something deeper about the story and the character.

Remember, unpredictable choices are not random for the sake of being random. They still need to be connected to the event of a scene, an aspect of your character and the work you've done. Unpredictable choices may seem to exist or come about by chance, but they are not, because they are rooted in the work you've done.

Please note that many actors will make unpredictable choices in their scene work that don't heighten or support the story and their character. Those choices come across more as them trying to be clever and interesting versus being authentic and interested.

When used correctly, unpredictable choices are a valuable part of story crafting and character development so that you keep the audience engaged from beginning to end.

Call to Action:

Who do you know in your universe that is unpredictable and makes random choices that can sometimes turn out positively or not so positively?

As you reflect on your most unpredictable friends and colleagues, write about what you learned from them in your journal.

The Deviant Condition of a Character

Deviant:

1. Abnormal, unnatural, irregular, unusual behavior.

When we're looking at deviant behavior as a tool for an actor to figure out the personality, habits and routines of a character or to explain the reasons why the character does what they do, we are looking for a pathological condition that deviates from the norm.

For instance, let's examine the deviant behavior of something that I know well: drug addiction. If you look at the reality of what addiction is, there is a cycle to it. The addiction cycle is composed of three components: obsession (thinking and obsessing about something), compulsion (acting on that obsession) and spiritual bankruptcy (the shame as a result of the action).

For example, if you're an addict, (or playing one), you're fixated on the fact that you don't feel well. You're depressed and feeling low. Stage one of the addiction cycle is kicking in. You think about how bad off you are and how you need a drink. And you say, "No, listen, I shouldn't be drinking. I don't want to. I don't want to drown my sorrows because it won't do me any good."

But you can't stop thinking about that drink. The more you think about how good it will make you feel, the more reasonable the idea becomes. Then, the second stage of compulsion kicks in. You act on your compulsion. You take a drink. Once you start going down that slippery slope, there is no stopping that train. Your compulsion takes over. One is too many, and a thousand is not enough. You drink until your actions precipitate behavior that is regrettable—sometimes disastrous. The results leave you in a state of spiritual bankruptcy or shame. You have now entered the third stage of addiction. You feel bad because you've probably done something or behaved in a way that is not good for you, anybody around you or the people who love you.

The character's deviant behavior is revealed through the behavior associated with the condition. In this case, the obsessive overthinking and dramatization of their psychological state might activate behaviors and physical reactions, such as pacing back and forth, dry mouth, nervous hands and manically searching for where the bottles are hidden.

So, deviant behavior goes back to the definition of abnormal, unnatural, irregular and unusual behavior. If you look at a person's normal behavior when things seem to be going well vs. when things are topsy-turvy—when things are painful, and they're fighting the desire to drink—the pathology of the character is where the reality of this disease kicks in.

An important note: the struggle with addiction doesn't have to be overt. It can be subtle, even when a character's life is out of control. In this case, you find that deviant behavior is a coping mechanism that an individual develops to help manage emotions they are incapable of processing or that are overwhelming.

Call to Action:

What consistent behavioral patterns have you observed from family members, friends or coworkers that seem odd, abnormal or self-destructive? In your opinion, what do you think is the cause of it?

Take notes in your journal when you see deviant behavior in action. What are the "tells" (behaviors) you notice that indicate something isn't "normal"?

Reflective Delay

Reflective Delay:
1. A period of deliberation that impedes or hinders.

Legendary actor, director and acting teacher Konstantin Stanislavski spoke about "reflective delay," and Milton mentioned it in his work. I have found reflective delay to be a key concept in acting. It separates actors from people.

Actors know too much. On the other hand, people do not know the answer to things most of the time, because life happens in the present moment. There is no script to follow. You can't anticipate what will happen next when you wake up and deal with life. When you go to the supermarket and engage with the cashier, no one gives you instructions that say, hey, this is how your exchange is gonna go. Sometimes, you don't know how to respond to certain interactions. You may be shocked, appalled, put off, frightened, angry or happy. And you might need a moment to process and deal with your emotions before responding.

For example, a woman got her tubes tied twenty years ago, so she for sure knows that kids are not in her future. She goes to the doctor one day, only to discover that she is pregnant. The actor reacts immediately with the appropriate amount of surprise and shock. On the other hand, a *person* is speechless for untold amounts of time, trying to process this impossibility.

A reflective delay occurs when processing new information and related emotions. People pause to reflect all the time.

Actors know too much because they have a script. They react immediately and automatically because they anticipate the lines or moments in a story. They can be on page one in a scene, but their focus is already on the emotional breakdown on page five. Many actors do not include that vital moment of processing the information they receive from another actor, and the feelings they are experiencing from that information. Instead, they are eager to jump to an emotional response or their lines.

One actor says to another actor, "I've been cheating on you with your best friend." And the other actor quickly responds, sometimes cutting off their scene partner before they finish their line. However, did this information land on the actor? Are they processing this powerful, revealing information to formulate a response that reflects what they just received?

In acting, you must process the information you receive because, in real life, people do that all the time. In our approach to acting, we want actors to be a specific person in a specific place, having a specific experience. When you process information, it affects your emotional state and behavior. It impacts when and how you say your line.

When an actor receives information, they are impacted by a period of deliberation that impedes or hinders them for some time. Through that experience of reflective delay, they can react more organically and truthfully, because they cannot respond until they first process the information.

Some students ask, "How long should my reflective delay be?" It depends on the gravity and importance of the information you receive from the other character. Or it depends on the situation, circumstance and your *Imagination*. It's often also influenced by the relationship the characters share. You can explore all of these things in the rehearsal process, or you can use the memory of your own experience. No matter the length of the reflective delay, the key is to process the information before responding.

I remember when I was in Australia to do a show called *Hotel Story*. I was the first Black actor to star in a series in Australia, and it was a big deal in 1976. One day, after a long shoot, my coworkers and I decided to go out for drinks. They left ahead of me, and I told them I'd grab a cab and meet them at the bar.

Well, I forgot that the traffic flow in Australia is on the opposite side of the street.

I jumped out of the taxi, looked to the left as you do in America, and saw nothing coming, so I started running across the street. Suddenly, I heard tires screeching so loudly and sharply that the noise felt like it was cutting right through the center of my body. I finished running across the street, opened the door, and went to the bar where the guys sat.

One of my new friends exclaimed, "Oh my God, we thought that was you. That was the scariest thing we've ever heard."

I said, "Yeah, that shit had to be close. I didn't see the car, but I felt it." And then, I excused myself to go to the restroom.

After I peed and went to wash my hands, I looked in the mirror, and then it hit me: *That car could not have come any closer; it's a miracle I'm not dead.* And I passed out right there on the floor. That is an example of reflective delay.

If you were playing me as a character, I would encourage you to apply the concept of reflective delay and see how long you could hold off the urge to play the emotion in the scene. The longer you could prolong it, the more interesting the scene. If you had said to the director, "I don't know that I would have that moment right away. It probably happens after I get out of the bathroom," the director probably would have said, "No, it's too long. That is not believable." When, in fact, that is precisely what happened. So, trust me, don't be afraid to have your ideas and be willing to fight for them.

Call to Action:

Recall an incident in your life that was so shocking that you didn't know how to react. How long did it take you to respond? And what did you say or do when you reacted?

As you write down the details of this experience, try to remember the nuances. In my story about almost being hit by a car, I vividly recall each beat (greeting my friends, excusing myself to the restroom, peeing, turning on the water to wash my hands, etc.). Those specifics can help you truly understand reflective delay.

Assets and Liabilities

Everyone in life is made up of qualities known as assets and liabilities. These qualities make up the 360 degrees of who we are as individuals. Assets are qualities people generally view as favorable and desirable (enthusiasm, kindness, passion, hard work, leadership skills, fearlessness, etc.). Liabilities are those qualities people consider negative or dark (anger, rage, jealousy, greed, victim, follower, weird, selfish, etc.). The combination creates the yin and yang in you. Yin and yang represent duality, or the idea that two opposite characteristics can coexist and complement each other. As an artist, you must be able to access each color in your emotional palette, be it light or dark. No human being is on one side or the other. You are a compilation of both.

For example, one of the things I really hate to admit is that I am jealous. I'm too cool to be jealous. Not! I'm so damn jealous from time-to-time. My green-eyed monster generally doesn't serve me in life. However, jealousy works for me if I'm playing a character. If I identify that the character is jealous, I can lend what I understand about jealousy to the character. I can paint with that color to make the character more specific and personal. If I can access the darker side of myself and manage that side of me, then it makes me a better actor. I have nothing to hide in the service of my art. I will not be afraid to paint boldly with these darker colors and reveal something powerful about the character I'm playing and the story I'm telling.

The same applies to accessing and managing your lighter side. Assets, if not managed, can turn into liabilities. Others can take advantage of a person's inclination towards being nice or wholehearted. For example, one of my assets is that I'm generous. I rarely say no. I give freely and happily, but sometimes, the receiver doesn't appreciate the gift. They've taken the thing that I gave them and trashed it. That is painful. So, your lighter side needs to be managed as well.

All of our light and dark emotions—our emotional circle—need to be managed. But it's the dark that people are most afraid of. It needs to be managed most because that's one of the more valuable parts of your creative ability to paint a character richly.

Assets and Liabilities
Discussion with Students

A student has just finished doing a cold stand-up on stage. Richard talks to them about leaning into all of the colors in their arsenal and the value of utilizing them in their artistic work.

RICHARD

The things that you are trying to avoid are the things that would really help provide more colors on your palette. For example, a painter utilizes a palette with all of these colors on it that they can paint with. Blue. A little red. Mix red and yellow. As an actor, the amount of colors on your palette helps provide you with the various emotions that you can put into a character. These colors are the various parts of yourself, both light and dark, the day and night of yourself, that you can use in your work. There are 24 hours in a day: *12 Hours of Light and 12 Hours of Darkness*. All of those colors are important in creating art. Now, the dark is just as important as the light. No person is just one thing. For example, Dave Chappelle said that Will Smith played the perfect man for 24 years until he wasn't anymore at the Oscars. And I'm just looking at the joke of it because I happen to have a great admiration for Will Smith. I just think he did a bad thing. He made a bad mistake. It doesn't make him a bad person.

So, those colors you are trying to avoid are things you need as an artist. The colors that you suppress are the very things that are going to give you contradiction and shading in your characters. Those colors are going to give you a sense of danger. They will allow you to be evil, angry, rageful, mischievous, jealous, deceitful—if those colors exist for you. They are just as important as you being kind, considerate, wise and smart. All of those things are the sum total. We need that part of you that you're trying to stifle. What we also need, and art has a way of doing this, is a way of giving you access to express emotions that other people can relate to and say, "Oh shit. I understand that character. I understand their desire to do that. I understand that pain."

If it wasn't for art, I don't know where the hell I would be. I don't know what I would do. Look, I've been to Vietnam. Nobody decompressed me when I came back. I didn't sit down with somebody who could talk me down from PTSD. I was the medic who dealt with bodies that were blown up. I was so desensitized to it that a dead body could be there, blown up, and I'm saying, "Yeah, man. You see this right here? This is the pancreas. And here's the stomach. Look at the gall bladder. The heart."

Ain't nobody said to me, "So how'd you feel about looking at that dead body when it was still warm? How'd you feel about putting your friend's leg back together when a tank ran him over? And you cut his pants open, and there were 10,000 lice and crabs all over his body, and you still had to put his body back together? How'd you feel when you picked up your friend's hand that was blown off, and he was a guitar player?"

But I could put all those experiences and all the other traumas I've been through into my art. I would be stark-raving mad if I wasn't an artist because I get to put it in the work. And when I do, other people can then relate to it. So, I encourage you to learn how to manage everything you're trying to suppress in life and pour it into your artistic work instead.

Call to Action:

Create two columns on a page in your journal or on an Excel spreadsheet. In the left column, list all of your assets. In the right column, list all of your liabilities. Be completely honest with yourself. Leave nothing out.

As you review those two lists, jot notes about how you might use each item in your work. Notice how your liabilities can start looking more like assets and vice versa.

Assessing Your Own Work

Another staple of my teaching is objectively and cleanly assessing your work. For most of our lives, we depend on others for validation or approval because we don't know any better. We were taught that our value derived from what others told us. Your teachers, parents, aunts and uncles, neighborhood and culture told you what was right and wrong. Things were thumbs up or thumbs down. Other people shaped and framed your value system.

Have you ever heard the expression, "Don't look at your work because it will confuse you"? That is one of the most asinine things I've ever heard because how do you tell a painter not to look at their art? How do you tell a writer not to read their writing?

As an actor, you have to be able to look at your work to determine its value for you. By seeing your work, you can shape it yourself and understand it so you'll know how to grow from it. You must get used to looking at yourself and embracing your assets and liabilities on screen. You must accept your flaws and get used to looking at the less-than-perfect aspects of yourself, as well as all the beauty and greatness that is there. Your crooked nose speaks to millions of people with crooked noses, and you represent hope for them.

Being able to assess your work properly is especially vital when you are working on a set. If you have done your homework and show up with a clear idea of your concept or product, you're better prepared to understand when your performance does not meet the standard you know you are capable of. If you've done the necessary research for the character and have sufficiently built an understanding of who this person is, when you show up to the set, you're ready to deliver your product. Now, of course, your vision has to pass through the lens of the director's vision. Through communication, you mutually create a collaboration of ideas and a character portrayal that is satisfying to both of you.

This preparation allows you to discern whether each take delivers the story you want to tell. You can tell what worked really well and you can also tell the parts you need to tweak. When you're working with an actor's director, (someone who understands performance and has the sensibility to help you make stronger and better choices and go further), then you're able to operate with a sense of trust.

For example, when working with a director whose experience comes from being a DP (Director of Photography) who knows how to shoot a beautiful movie and not much about directing actors, I know I have to depend on myself to curate a performance. That's why it's my mission to help actors have the ability to direct themselves if need be.

Call to Action:

At the end of the day, when you're on set, make it a habit to write an assessment in your journal about how the day went. See if you can first acknowledge everything you did well before pointing out the things that didn't go well.

The Acting Lexicon Review

1. Event (Obvious and Real)
2. To What Degree/Extent?
3. The Moment Before
4. Behavior
5. Be Your Best Self
6. Inner and Outer Life
7. Humor
8. Moment to Moment
9. Mother's Gold Cross
10. God is in the Details
11. Objectives
12. Unpredictable Choices
13. The Deviant Condition of a Character
14. Reflective Delay
15. Assets and Liabilities
16. Assessing Your Own Work

Call to Action:

Create a cheat sheet in your journal that lists each item in The Acting Lexicon with a one-line description. This exercise challenges you to create clarity and understanding for each item.

Acting Exercises

Creating an Environment with a Crisis

One of the cornerstones of my teaching is to be a specific person in a specific place having a specific experience. All the great actors in TV, film and theater look like people living and operating in a specific environment. It doesn't feel like they're acting. "Creating an Environment with a Crisis" is an exercise that teaches actors how to do that, and it's the first exercise I require from my students.

The first step is to duplicate an environment that would be in your own familiar space. For example, if you decided to duplicate your kitchen, you would bring as many things as possible from your kitchen to recreate that same environment on stage. The more specific and detailed you make your environment, the better.

The next step is to create a clear event by doing an activity you are highly invested in. For instance, if you were painting, you would work on a picture of something you're genuinely interested in. You're not just painting by the numbers or in a superficial, disengaged way. The purpose of this is for the activity to ground you in reality. You are doing something real, rather than pretending or "acting" something. You are engaged moment-to-moment in your activity.

As a result, you start to believe in your experience. I don't care what the activity is. If the activity is folding clothes, and the event is that you've washed your clothes for the week, be intentional about folding those clothes.

When the event of your activity is clear, you start living in your environment as a person would. You are fully committed to what you're doing, which maintains the level of tension that keeps you invested.

Once you are fully absorbed in your activity, you receive a phone call. You answer the phone, and the caller delivers tragic news. Whether or not you know the caller, don't plan the crisis or rehearse your response ahead of time. Let your **Imagination** create the crisis on the spot so that your experience on stage is spontaneous, organic and moment-to-moment.

For instance, if you have recreated your living room and are folding clothes at the end of a long week, the last thing you want to do is your chores. But you know if you don't do it now, you'll never get it done. So, even though you're hating every minute, you're still folding everything properly so it's easy to put away—put the towels with the towels, the underwear with the underwear, etc.

Then, one of the stage managers calls your phone and you answer it. Your **Imagination** activates and spontaneously creates a crisis that the caller delivers "I regret to inform you that your spouse has been in an accident, and they are in a serious condition." This is shocking news, to say the least.

My first question is, how do human beings react when they receive tragic news? One size doesn't fit all, that's for sure. Every human being is different, and it depends on the individual's personality, but let's look at some possible aspects of what occurs:

- Do you believe what you're hearing?
- Who's calling?
- Are you in shock?
- What behaviors occur?

  o Shaking?
  o Nervousness?
  o Crying?
  o Numbness?
  o Speechless?
  o Feeling faint?
  o Stuttering?
  o Heart rate increases?
  o Blood pressure soars?
  o Tightness in your chest?

Depending on your relationship with the person involved in the crisis, (mother, father, sister, brother, wife, husband, lover etc.), the degree of your engagement during that phone call will determine the evaluation of this new event. Preceding the phone call, your ability to fully engage in that initial event sets you up to embrace anything else that comes along.

The key to this exercise is to find an event that highly interests you. The more interested you are, the greater your experience. Belief in your experience will create deeper involvement in the event. This immersion in the process will set you up to be fully invested, so when the crisis appears, you are completely submerged in the experience. You aren't trying to convince yourself of anything because you are already deep in belief.

How does this translate into work on the set with other actors? Let's say that you have a four-page scene, and there's an emotional moment near the end of the scene. The tendency is to pay attention to the expectation of the emotional demands of that upcoming moment. Throughout the scene, 20-50 percent of your attention will be focused on the hope and prayer that you will be emotionally full enough when you get to that moment. You'll think, "Oh, here it comes on the next page. This is where I have to cry." Your focus will be on what you fear, as opposed to being focused on the present moment of just folding the clothes, which you hate. You can't look in two directions at the same time. They will both suffer.

"Creating an Environment with a Crisis" helps you to hone in on the reality of the moment that you're in. You're not anticipating the crisis or the big emotional moment related to the phone call. And now, it is just a matter of you continuing to seduce yourself in the crisis and letting it play out naturally, like any other person would.

Call to Action:

On holidays like Thanksgiving or Christmas, when families have gathered to enjoy the festivities, there are usually one or several outliers in the group who are sure to cause havoc. Observe the environment during the event and how people handle the crisis when it occurs. Later in your journal, describe what you observed. How did you handle it?

Can You Live Comfortably in the Box?

Can you reach a level of relaxation where you are present, aware and open to your sensibilities? Where you're willing to see and be seen, and therefore able to perceive? Often, you have tension in parts of your body that you're unaware of. We all do.

As a teacher, I constantly observe how my students hold themselves—and their stress. It's evident in how they walk and carry themselves. I can see the tension in body language and posture. They might have a curve in their spine, where one shoulder is higher or lower than the other, making them lean slightly to one side. Sometimes, people have a nervous reaction when being observed. There's noticeable neck tension, which I can see in how their heads move. Maybe their hands, legs and feet jump repeatedly when they sit, like they're plugged into an electric socket. Human beings have all kinds of tics.

Functioning on the highest level possible as an actor requires the ability to unwind. When you are relaxed, you are more present. You can better access your emotions, follow impulses and positively impact your fellow actors.

The ***Can You Live Comfortably in the Box?*** exercise is an important tool for achieving a state of relaxation. It helps you to decompress and let go of any tics, allowing you to create in a more free and effortless way.

The first part of the exercise helps you identify your stress signals. You stand alone on stage, looking into the audience, while I walk around you to check for tension and tics. During this check-in, I may do a few different things:

- Unlock your knees to release tension.
- Stop you from tapping your leg with your fingers or swaying from side-to-side.
- Lift your arm and let it go to see if it hangs in the air or drops like dead weight back to your side. (If it hangs in the air, that signifies tension. I will keep lifting your arm and encouraging you to relax until the arm drops like dead weight.)

By checking in, I am getting you to be pliable, open, present and free from tension, tics and any other signs of stress. When your body moves involuntarily, it's a tell you're experiencing tension. Your ability to be present evaporates and scatters in various directions. You inadvertently block any emotional responses or instincts that may come up. In your artistic work, you want to access and invite these elements freely.

Once I find that you are relaxed and present, the next part of this exercise is for you to sing a song you have chosen. It is not about the singing sounding nice. This doesn't matter. It's about communicating the song to the people in the room and connecting with them without self-judgment, consideration or tension.

The point of this part of the exercise is to train you to relax when you're in a high-stress situation, like when you're "in the box" (a reference to a close-up on camera). In the box, your movement is minimal. And it becomes easy to start letting tics and tension enter the mix because of the pressure to deliver or to be interesting on camera. You may begin fidgeting because you don't believe you are enough. You must be comfortable and relaxed to deliver an emotional experience within this tight frame.

As you sing, connect with your diaphragm so that you sing in your true voice. As a kid, I thought Johnny Mathis had a beautiful voice. So, singing to me equated to singing like how Johnny Mathis sang. Using that as a reference, I would try replicating his voice—a no-win situation. If you're singing outside of yourself, you are vocalizing with tension.

While you sing, I continue to check for tension and tics. At some point, I will ask you to sing out more loudly. Sometimes, this additional push will help you tap into feelings you wouldn't normally access. Doing something vulnerable, like singing, can be liberating. We spend a great deal of our lives protecting ourselves. No one wants to feel pain. The difference is that in art, we have to be able to access those vulnerabilities and bear them to the world.

After you are present, relaxed and singing with abandon, I tell you to march around the stage and sing. I then instruct you to put an enemy underneath your feet, causing you to stomp around the stage. This physical activity sometimes allows the body to open up and relax more. When this happens, the emotion comes, and your real voice might kick in.

Then, I will ask you to skip light-heartedly around the stage (while singing) to continue freeing the body up. The next step is to have you stand in place and dance wildly, with no particular form, to loosen the body up even more. After you finish dancing, I will ask you to stand in the center of the stage again, look out at the audience, and reconnect with them. Finally, I will ask you to sing one more time.

Once you can do all those things successfully, you will have grown in your ability to access a wide range of emotions—many that you wouldn't have otherwise had in your repertoire. You are different by the time you get to the end of this exercise. You will hold yourself without any tension or tics. You will sing with your true voice and not some idea of what your singing should sound like. You will be more emotionally vulnerable and available. You see the audience and connect with them with greater clarity and certainty.

We are so used to carrying our tension and holding on to our feelings, ideas and points of view that we don't notice how inhibited we are. Once we get past all that, we can be present, willing to see and be seen, and therefore able to perceive.

Call to Action:

Karaoke is a great test to determine a person's ability to relax under pressure. Challenge yourself to partake in karaoke with your friends and see if you can find a way to relax regardless of your singing skill. It's more about your ability to be present and in your body as much as possible. Try it.

What's the Real Truth?

When you see a piece of art that you truly love and it moves you, there is a resonant truth about it. You relate because it touches you on a personal level.

Everything you do in art should be personal. I don't care if you're singing a song, doing stand-up, acting in a farce, doing improv or reciting Shakespeare. I don't care whether you play a lover, fighter or killer. Everything you do as an actor should be personal because it starts with you. You are the canvas and the work emanates from within. You bring forth your experiences and knowledge so that you can play your characters in a specific, connected and authentic way.

One of my favorite quotes on the importance of actors bringing their unique interpretations and emotional experiences to their work is attributed to Konstantin Stanislavski:

"Never be afraid of an author. An actor is a free artist. You want to create an image that is different from the author's.

When the two images—the author's and the actor's—fuse into one, then a true artistic work is created."

Before I give you the low-down on an excellent exercise to understand what it means to be authentic in your work, I'll share a personal story:

I'm a former Catholic. I was a Catholic until I was sixteen years old. My uncle and I were driving down a street in Lafayette, Louisiana when I saw a beautiful cathedral.

RICHARD

Uncle Cliff, pull over. I want to go see this beautiful stained glass inside this church.

UNCLE CLIFF

You can't go in there.

RICHARD

Why not? It's a Catholic Church.

UNCLE CLIFF

It's a *white* Catholic Church.

RICHARD
(devastated)

But wait, I don't understand. It's a house of God. I'm an altar boy. I might even be a priest someday. So how come I can't go in there?

UNCLE CLIFF

Son, if you go into that church to look around, they will carry you out on a stretcher.

As we drove by that cathedral, I remember looking at it until it disappeared in the distance. And when I turned back around in my seat, I was no longer Catholic.

The one thing I loved about the Catholic Church was the sacrament of confession. I appreciated going into a confessional booth and saying, "Bless me, Father, for I have sinned." Then, it was all about trying to figure out a way to explain to Father Murphy that I did "bad" things, like masturbating. That was a very tough thing to do as a kid. But to be able to confess was a blessing—even though Father Murphy gave me 50 Hail Marys and 50 Acts of Contrition as a result. So, I'd go into the chapel, kneel and pray for 35 minutes. The act of praying was a form of amends for the guilt or shame I had absorbed, and it allowed me to feel better about myself. It was a form of forgiveness.

The "What's the Real Truth?" exercise serves a similar function. It provides a way for you to confront the deeply held secrets in your life because **We Are Only as Sick as Our Biggest Secret.** We all have life experiences that act as a filter. Certain things that make us feel bad about ourselves. Things that we hide, things that we don't want to share with anyone. These secrets limit us because they're often a source of embarrassment or self-loathing. Remember: **Guilt is "I Made a Mistake." Shame is "I Am a Mistake."**

It is very difficult for you to be a free-flowing artist when confronted by those pockets of shame. You don't want to venture into those feelings because they may expose you and show the world how grotesque you really are.

What I know from personal and professional experience is that **Freedom is Having Nothing to Hide.**

The "What's the Real Truth?" exercise is an opportunity to alleviate the weight of long-held secrets. For example, I might tell the story I just wrote above, about when I decided I was no longer Catholic.

This exercise empowers you to creatively share a story on stage or film to confront a demon. You're not forcing the story.

You're just telling it, allowing the narrative to occur to you as you share it. And hopefully, by the time you finish your monologue, you will have gotten to the other side of this challenging thing you've confronted.

When you tell this story, it becomes some of your most personal work, thus becoming your best work as an actor. You take a look at an overwhelming situation, clear-eyed and honest. Done right, you are never more real than you are in this exercise—which is a great way to look at it, especially if it's filmed. You'll see how moment-to-moment you are. By confronting something that powerful, your acting will never be better. It can become a standard for you to aspire to match for the rest of your career.

Actors tend to discount the exercise by saying, "But this doesn't count as acting because I told a true story." As I tell my students, it *does* count because the story came from you, and you had a personal experience with it. That is what acting is all about. The key is to take that same experience and behavior from your story and apply it to your work on a script someone else wrote. It should feel like you wrote those words yourself, and your performance should be as intimate as when you delivered your personal story.

The "What's the Real Truth?" exercise is a valuable tool for creatively confronting complex scenes. It helps you understand how to be simple, moment-to-moment and connected with that experience.

So, notice the behaviors the experience elicits. During my confessional experience, for instance, I remember sweating, my hands shaking, my voice trembling, feeling sick to my stomach, on the verge of tears and wanting to disappear. If I play a character going through a similar emotional experience or situation, I can lend these behaviors to them so that my work becomes specific and personal. In other words, "Like the time when I…"

Call to Action:

The next time you confide in a friend, your therapist, your pastor or someone you trust, challenge yourself to be as transparent as possible, making it a point to get to the other side of the problem. Write about your experience in your journal.

To the Nth Degree

What is the nth degree? To the nth degree is an idiom that means "to the utmost or as much or as far as possible, leaving no stone unturned."

"To the Nth Degree" is one of the most fascinating acting exercises. What makes it so intriguing? I have seen nth degree exercises that have been absolutely startling and transformational, that were so complete and experienced that you would have thought you were seeing an apparition. It's scary how powerful this exercise can be.

The nth degree exercise is where you choose a photograph to help you tap into and discover a particular reality, essence or quality of a character you are portraying or a quality you want to discover in yourself as an actor. Perhaps you are looking to find the qualities of an older or younger person, or someone with a certain range of emotion. The process of looking outside of yourself or deeply into yourself frees an artist from being limited by their own considerations. The photograph guides you into a truth and life that you may not be able to achieve without it.

At its best, this exercise is transformative and spiritual—spiritual in the sense that the actors evoked the character's spirit. The core concept of this exercise is for the actor to duplicate the photograph to the nth degree, get into the precise position, and then get out of the way. This is not about acting. It's not even about you and your ego at this point. It's about allowing the spirit of the person in the photograph to take over during this exercise. The more you allow the person to take over and emerge, the more you will experience and be in belief.

In this exercise, you are dealing with specifics and details, **Asking the Next Question**, using personal objects and going to the nth degree to duplicate the contents of the photograph and bring that character to life. The whole picture dictates the way a character emerges from the actor.

After you do all the research and work and arrive at class completely prepared down to the most minute detail—all done up with hair, makeup and wardrobe, including any props—you are ready to take that journey. If the person in the photo was seated in a chair, you find as similar a chair as possible. The same type of chair should be the same height as the one in the picture. This is crucial because, in this exercise, the actor must be in the exact position of the person in the photograph. Not similar or close to the position, but the precise position. All elements (the tilt of her head, how they're holding the cane, etc.) must be exact.

Once the actor is in the precise position, I ask them to make a sound. The reason is simple: Since the head is in an exact position, it dictates the sound from the actor's mouth. So, for example, if your head is bent slightly to the lower left, and your chin is to your neck, you might get a deeper, more guttural tone. That sound begins the journey of bringing the character in the photo to life. You don't question or judge it. It coaxes out something different from your own being.

Then, I ask the actor to make another sound. And then another. The next step is for the actor to speak. How they communicate is influenced by the position of the person's head and body, how they're sitting or standing and the energy the actor seeks and receives from the character. Without judgment, the actor allows the voice to emerge. The voice will lead the actor.

If you want to keep this exercise expanding, add another person on stage so you can start a conversation. Or, the teacher can engage the actor. If you do this, you'll get a sense of the character's point of view, passion, **Humor, Charm and Irony.** You get the invaluable opportunity to experience how the person in the photograph feels, thinks and responds.

Here's how I usually continue this exercise: After the actor has been speaking for a while and I feel the character is doing the leading, I let them go off on their own. In other words, if the actor is in belief and having an experience that is not led by their acting ability but by the inspiration of the spirit coming through them, I step back. Eventually, I encourage the actor to walk around the stage and interact with other people.

If the actor loses the character or falls out of belief, they go back to square one, and I'll reset them in the precise position so they can start over and take that journey again.

The nth degree exercise is an invaluable tool to help an actor create a specific reality and belief about a character they seek to understand and master. It's a key to what's possible in terms of creating a fully realized character through nth degree work.

Call to Action:

This exercise is usually done with someone helping to place the person in the exact position as the individual in the picture. Find a photo using the criteria laid out in this chapter. Do all you can to duplicate the image to the nth degree. See if you can turn over every possible stone to fulfill the task of creating a valuable and wonderful character.

Cold Exercises

Cold exercises are a methodology I use extensively in my teaching. I assign cold stand-ups, songs, improvisations, walking, monologues, laugh/cry/laugh and drunk physical state exercises—all without giving people any notice. One of the reasons I like to employ this particular methodology is because the actor is not prepared, so they're not influenced by preconceived ideas or notions about what should or should not happen.

For instance, when you call upon an actor to do a cold stand-up routine, they immediately go through a long list of self-examinations: *Oh my God, I don't want to fail. I can't think of anything. I don't know what to say. I'm embarrassed. I feel exposed. People are going to think that I am not talented. I'm not funny.*

The list of things that go through a person's mind depends on their personality, who they are and how they were raised. So many filters pop up that prevent them from being present and **On Go.**

Cold exercises are not rehearsed or planned. There's no blueprint for what you're getting ready to do. You're starting straight from scratch. You have to rely on your instincts, impulses and thoughts. You have to deal with the whole concept of embarrassment—that feeling of being hot and uncomfortable.

Actress Rosalind Russell once said, **"Acting is Standing Up Naked and Turning Around Very Slowly."** Part of the conditioning that prepares you to live under that hot light and manage that sense of embarrassment and exposure is getting to a place where you recognize and feel you are enough.

One of the most challenging things to develop is that muscle—the knowledge, confidence and self-awareness that you are enough. Where I stand right now is enough. I know everything I need to know, and I have access to my complete range of assets and liabilities, and I can call upon them at any given time. And I'm **Not Going To Let My Creativity Pass Through the Lens of Someone Else's Morality.**

That is a very steep ask because most of us have grown up with the voices of **K-SHIT FM** playing in our heads. **K-SHIT FM** records and plays all of those negative thoughts and comments you've collected along the way—things that make us think we are not enough, less than, grotesque, imperfect, that we don't know what we know and that we don't have any talent. This station tends to play the loudest when you are in the spotlight of the unknown.

My job as an educator and artist is to help you create a new station that I call **K-ART FM.** This station is the counterpoint to **K-SHIT FM. K-ART FM** has positive affirmations, memories of wins and successful actions and a knowingness that you are enough. This new station results from being around and supported by your selected and curated family: your tribe, community and strategy group, which consistently confirms your value. This alternative station encourages you to live in your discomfort, be present and breathe, discover your truth in a moment and allow that to be the moment and truth you live in.

One of my favorite parables is a Cherokee legend called "The Two Wolves":

One evening, a little boy comes to his grandfather, angry that another child has wronged him. The grandfather says, "I understand; I have sometimes felt the same. But hate is like drinking poison and wishing your enemy would die. So, let me tell you a story:

'Two wolves live inside of me. One is good and means no harm. He doesn't get upset when someone says or does something to offend him but doesn't mean to. He only fights when it's justified and necessary. The other wolf is full of rage. He fights at the slightest provocation. While he is filled with anger, his fury changes nothing.

There is a terrible fight between the two wolves, and it's for the right to dominate my spirit. In fact, we all have these two wolves living inside of us, engaging in the same struggle.'"

The little boy pipes up and asks his grandfather, "Which wolf will win?"

The wise grandfather simply replies, "The one you feed."

The two wolves represent our opposing emotions and attitudes. The "bad" wolf symbolizes negative emotions like fear, anger and envy, while the "good" wolf represents positive emotions like joy, peace and love. As the grandfather suggests, the outcome of this internal struggle depends on the choices you make.

This story reminds you that you have control over your attitudes and emotions. It encourages you to nurture the positive aspects of your character and not let negativity consume you. It's a timeless lesson in personal responsibility and self-awareness.

My experience as a teacher has shown me that, in most cases, if you think you are not funny, have nothing to say, or are affected by the voluminous negative voices stored on your **K-SHIT FM** station, you will discover that there is an alternative station to listen to. **K-ART FM** helps you embrace being present and focusing on the positive.

Once you have the patience to find that thing that interests you, you will find a way to communicate that. You're not trying to be interesting, but are interested in that subject or memory. As you tell it how you feel or experience it, you will discover that you are honestly looking at something, which ultimately winds up being true for you. And that truth has tremendous **Humor, Charm and Irony**. Little by little, you discover that your talent is much greater than you had ever imagined.

Say the subject is relationships the first time you do cold stand-up. You start talking about the craziness of relationships. Within five minutes, you have said five different things about relationships. Later, when you listen to the recording of what you have said and make notes, you can begin to extrapolate *(deduce, envision, project)* those things. You take it to the next level, and before you know it, you have a 10-15 minute set about relationships. And if you continue to do cold stand-up, you will develop a whole set the same way with different subjects.

The same concept of extrapolation applies when you do a cold personal monologue. After reflecting on it, you discover that not only is it interesting, but it's also worthy of something bigger. You start developing it. You turn it into a short film, a series idea or even a documentary. The beauty of this is that you are creating these things out of your own story and sense of truth. This is why I always say cold exercises are the most valuable practices for an artist.

Cold Stand-up (Comedy)

The word "comedy" is intimidating. You feel pressure to be funny. You may even compare yourself to professional comics or someone who was funny in your family while minimizing your sense of humor and thus belittling your point of view. Ultimately, you have to decide where you are looking.

When asked to do cold stand-up, are you looking at the glass being half empty or half full? Are you looking at all the things that can go wrong, or are you looking at an opportunity to seize the room? Are you focusing on Uncle Bob, who told you years ago that you're not funny? Or are you remembering how embarrassing or awkward it was to stand up in front of people?

Those who look at the glass half-empty allow a state of embarrassment to take over. Embarrassment means to inhibit freedom of thought, speech, or action because of something which slows or confuses mental action; to block and prevent liberty of movement. You apologize for your existence. You shrink in size and retreat into the shadows.

You can't create art if you can't manage embarrassment. It comes with the territory.

However, if you look at the glass half full when you do a cold stand-up exercise, you will always deliver. I have never seen a student fail at cold stand-up when I have asked them to do it on the spot. You bypass any considerations and embarrassment you may feel because you trust that you are enough. You are willing to share the first story that pops into your head without judgment or criticism. And because of this, you find a unique point of view and personal connection to your story that ends up being quite funny. You are not trying to be funny or interesting. Instead, the comedy emanates naturally from the personal connection with the story you're telling. Cold stand-up is a great way to get out of your way and **Be On Go.** The more you do this in your art, the more present you will be in life.

Having possession of cold stand-up is also an important tool in the areas of politics, personality and craft. By developing this skill set and sharing stories unapologetically, you will duplicate that experience in the outside world. You can share stories at dinner parties, casting sessions or any place someone asks you to tell them something about yourself. Sharing stories and conversing effortlessly and confidently will help you build relationships at different places. People will like you, invite you back to other events and may even introduce you to opportunities.

Cold Stand-up Discussion

A student has just finished doing cold stand-up in class.

RICHARD

You've been doing cold stand-up for a number of years, right? What has it brought to your reality as an artist?

STUDENT 1

It's brought me confidence and freedom. It's helped me find my voice and my point of view. It's been a way for me to connect with people, know that I'm enough and know that, at any moment, I can think of something. I no longer question my ability to do cold stand-up, and I don't question my ability to deliver. For me, this exercise is not about being funny. I wasn't planning on talking about that topic with anyone. It's about being brave and being honest. The other thing is when I get called on in a class setting to do cold stand-up, it's helped me through challenging times. If I have really been struggling with something and can't get it out of my head, it's helped me get present, get real with it and then find the humor in it to get to the other side because humor is the gift of life.

RICHARD

Good. Anybody have any questions about what cold exercises are, what they do or what their value is?

STUDENT 2

I just want to make sure I understand the purpose of a cold exercise. This student didn't plan on talking about that. You just called her up to the stage. It wasn't rehearsed or planned. She just went off the cuff with it, correct?

RICHARD

Yeah, there's nothing planned about that. She was not scheduled to go up tonight. What it does is that it gives you, like she said, the confidence of yourself. To know that at any given moment, you can find the truth in being present, the humor in something and that you don't need to know absolutely everything. The answers will come to you in the moment.

STUDENT 2

I see.

RICHARD

And then to have the courage to say that thing you think is taboo or secret or scary or whatever. It's about being brave.

STUDENT 2

Thank you.

RICHARD

Somebody once said to Lucille Ball that she was really a funny person. And Lucille Ball said, "I'm not funny. What I am is brave." When you look at her work, you see the truth of that because of the fact that she did some really ridiculous things. Look at *I Love Lucy*. You will see bravery at its finest.

STUDENT 3

So, what's the best approach for people who have struggled with something like this when it comes to improv and stand-up? Is it better to tell a true story, or is it better to make something up?

RICHARD

Most of the stories told here are true. And if they're not, they feel like they're true. Do you know what I mean? People just come from a sense of truth. We have a comedy class, and all those comedians start with something personal on the first day of class. She just did this stand-up, which was recorded, by the way, and can be transcribed. And she can now start developing an act about aluminum deodorant armpits. Then, she talks about something else and repeats that same process. And one-by-one, she develops a half-hour set from stuff out of her life. You know your own life better than anything, and in reality, here's the thing: We don't know if that story is true. But she made us feel like it was. And that's the whole thing about comedy. So, if we can demystify the concept of comedy and take the onus off of having to be funny or a good joke teller, we can find our own sense of humor.

***

During another class, a student shares with Richard that she is creating a sitcom she is starring in. Their conversation leads to Richard having her do a cold stand-up on the spot.

STUDENT

I am currently working on a sitcom, and yes, the character is within my first wave of casting. I'm super proud because I presented my opening scene in my Professional Development class today!

The class cheers and applauds.

RICHARD

Okay, great. So you're trying to develop your comedy and your sense of humor.

STUDENT

I am.

RICHARD

And do you know where that is? Because comedy is not one thing. Look at any comedic series. Each one has its own zip code and its own genre. Personally, I never felt good about sitcoms—even though I eventually acted in them—where there's a laugh every five to seven lines. However, that's not where my heart went. But I also did shows like *The Days and Nights of Molly*

Dodd, which was a dramedy. And in one episode, you might get one laugh, but the whole episode leads up to that one laugh. And that laugh was fall-down dramatically funny. What made the show so much fun was that Molly would go off into different scenarios and fantasies. Her mother would say, "Molly, do you know what you should do?" And Molly would say, "What?" And then her mother would say something, and Molly would say, "Yeah." And then we were transported to this world of the 1950s or '60s. In one episode, she thought she wanted to be a cop, so she was in a ride-along with cops. And those scenarios and her experiences were usually hysterically funny. I played one of her boyfriends. David Strathairn, who is a wonderful actor, was the other boyfriend. Molly got pregnant and she had my baby. That was in the 1980s. That was new territory.

So, that kind of comedy was right in the heart of my sensibility. I loved that. Those other shows weren't my first choice. Whenever I got those scripts, I had to get over myself because I was like, "Oh shit. Here we go." So you have to understand the kind of comedy and your sense of humor, and as you develop that, you will know where that lives. And then, that will become second nature to you, which can become your ticket to the party.

STUDENT

Absolutely. I totally understand, and that is something I am working on—finding my sense of humor and being comfortable with it. Part of why I value the Professional Development Program so much is that I'm able to explore and be "corny." So yeah, that's part of the process of finding my voice and the angle of how I want my show to look, feel and sound.

RICHARD

Yeah, that's cool. So come up here and do some stand-up.

The student gets up on stage and does a cold stand-up. The class cheers and applauds when she finishes.

RICHARD

That was great. Very funny. There was a lot of material in there. You talked about probably five different subjects. If you took those subjects and did a deeper dive into each one: traveling, dating, being single, ghetto toast and the relationship with your mother, just be truthful and real. Each of those subjects has more of a reality to them. Work that and then build upon that material because it's building upon your truth. You're not trying to find jokes. You can find a way to make those stories funnier and find the joke by setting things up and paying them off. What I love about cold stand-up is that you can't think about it. It's coming organically from you, and these subjects are truthful. There's a whole exploration that can happen from that. So, for you to continue to explore will only help your project. Do you understand that?

STUDENT

Absolutely. Diving deeper is probably one of the areas that I have to really work on.

RICHARD

Yes, because that kind of authenticity pulls us into you. The artists you like the most, whether they're singers, dancers, actors or painters, are creating from a depth of truth that resonates across a universal spectrum. Because even though that's true for them, other people can see their pain or interest in the subject because it's relatable. So, your truth makes your work and your art relatable to others. What I want you to do is listen to this recording, take a look at what you talked about and build on that. Then, I want you to bring it back within a month. And then, a month later, I want you to do your set at a comedy club.

STUDENT

Okay, I can do that!

Call to Action:

Create an evening once a month where you invite your friends over to do cold stand-up. Each of you takes turns telling stories and finding the humor in them. Don't try to tell jokes. Just tell stories that interest you. All of you will find your own kind of funny.

Cold Song

Life and art are about connection. When we meet people, our first level of connection is the energy we carry, which is transmitted through our voice. We say hello. Whoever receives that hello has already learned so much about you from your energy and the sound of your voice. They can tell whether your hello is genuine. They can perceive confidence or uncertainty. They may even be able to tell if you're a mama's boy or a daddy's girl, a martyr or a hero and whether or not you're trying to be liked.

How does one perceive something so specific from a hello? A daddy's girl, for instance, learned to behave in a particular way to get her father's attention. Often, the voice is higher pitched, the behavior is mildly seductive and there's a sweet quality that isn't present when interacting with the mom. This woman might go into a default daddy's girl behavior pattern around men. Perceptive people can pick up on that—the same with the aforementioned archetypes.

As an artist, you must understand that your voice is your first line of communication. It says so much about who you are, what you think, your point of view and how you feel. It needs to be developed and trained. You must have mastery over your calling card. Your voice gets you through the door. How you communicate—and what's behind it—is everything. It affects all things moving forward. Your voice impacts how you get cast and whether you are believable in a particular role. For example, you won't be believable as a boss if you have a weak voice.

What me and my fellow teachers discern from doing a cold song is where someone is at with their voice. We can see if you are using your voice, breath and diaphragm properly so the sound reverberates through your chest. We can see if you produce enough breath. If you don't, your voice goes into your head, and you can sound nasal.

That said, a nasal quality can be very useful as a character type when you are in control and can produce it intentionally. Some people have had great careers with those types of voices, like Peter Lorre (of *Casablanca* and *The Maltese Falcon*). However, if that is the voice you default to, you aren't in control. If you can ground yourself in the sound produced from your diaphragm, you can create any voice you want for a character.

A cold song is assigned randomly and unexpectedly. This keeps everyone in the room on their toes, because you never know when you'll get called for a cold exercise.

After being called up, the person arrives on the stage or in the virtual window (if it's an online class), having no idea what to sing. The beauty of the exercise is that you start off a blank canvas, and you have to find a way to become present and grounded. Most people will initially focus on their fear, anxiety and lack of confidence. After studying with me for a while, they will learn that they are enough. They will be present and have the patience to just look around their universe until they think of a song they can sing. They will **Do Their Best and Forget the Rest**.

To understand the power of voice, think about a time when you had a television on in the background and heard a familiar voice—it's one of your favorite actors! That voice is very much a part of their brand because you recognize it anywhere.

The cold song is one way to discover where you are vocally, emotionally and spiritually. A good teacher will help you become aware of the difference between your natural, organic voice and the voice you developed to survive growing up.

Call to Action:

On the same night you perform cold stand-up, add a cold song to the mix. You just have to test your bravery.

Cold Improvisation

The word improvisation means spontaneity, lack of premeditation. It is a cold exercise by the very nature of this definition. Improv is used to create a sense of freedom. It allows you to unleash your **Imagination** and sharpens your ability to listen and be moment-to-moment. You can only rely on your creativity, self-determinism, instinct, perceptions and impulses. That requires a lot of trust. And the ability to make it up as you go along requires the willingness to imitate, simulate and pretend without judgment.

Let's say the prompt is you're a cowboy who was just thrown off a bucking horse. What are the possibilities? Are you dusty? Do you have a sore butt, back or shoulder? Are you cursing the horse? Are they chewing on tobacco? Trying to find their hat?

To imitate, simulate and pretend without judgment means you take one or more of those possibilities and immediately create the experience. Let's say you have a sore butt from being thrown. Physicalizing the ache will help you begin to believe the pain. Belief in the pain will enhance the experience and inspire other nuances to surface.

All of this is accomplished by diving into the depths of your **Imagination** without constraint. It does not have to come from an actual experience. Remember: imitate, simulate and pretend. If you dare to let loose, something organic may happen.

The use of improvisation in scene work is also valuable. Improvisation can help fill in unknown details of a character, such as their history, relationship with other people, subtext and hidden desires. When you explore the obvious event in a scene, improv can help you determine the real event. Remember, the obvious event is what the writer gives you. It is what the character says and what everyone sees on the surface. The real event is what is *not* said. Improvisation can help you determine the real event.

Call to Action:

In the same vein as the other cold exercises, as you explore with your cohorts, one of you can be the "director." Come up with a scenario for the other group members. It can start with two people in the improv, and the director can add people to complicate the situation. It can be fun! Notice that by doing these exercises, you are building a community of like-minded artists.

Cold Walking

Actors were once trained to be "triple threats." They were taught to become excellent singers and dancers—it was part of the required skill set to act on stage and film. Triple-threat actors always had work, because they knew their voice and body were part of their instrument.

Today, that isn't necessarily so. Yes, there are still triple threats out there, and many of these talented people come from universities with outstanding programs, like Howard, Yale, NYU and Julliard. But for the most part, the pool of actors with that skill set has declined tremendously. A lot of actors train only in television. They get a show on TV and don't have to use their voice or body because the mic is right there, and the camera will move for them.

When it comes to movement, actors are not as prepared. They don't live in their bodies very well. When you go to dance class, you learn to move, feel your body and express yourself physically. Consider some iconic actors: Denzel Washington has a purposeful walk that people find sexy, strong and confident. Through his body language, he communicates that he's a leader, and it even gives him a sense of danger. John Wayne walked with a cowboy's swagger. Sophia Loren and Marilyn Monroe each had their own iconic, seductive ways of walking. All these people live in their bodies—and their bodies are a language in itself.

When you are on screen and in real life, you want to make a statement with how you enter, leave and inhabit a scene. So, I devised a cold walking exercise.

The instruction is simple: Be present, and walk with as much freedom and certainty as possible. The actor's comfort and confidence are revealed almost instantly. After walking a couple of times around the stage, I start working with the actor, pointing out where they are holding tension and stress.

During this exercise, it's obvious how a person lives in their body (or not). This information is critical because when you are a guest star, or especially when you start playing lead characters, you must live in your body. Your confidence, or lack thereof, will be immediately apparent. When you are trained in truly inhabiting your body, you can communicate a range of qualities from cool and confident to desirable, shifty, anxious and much more.

If you feel detached from your body or unable to express yourself physically, consider taking a dance class to learn how to live well in your body.

Call to Action:

When you go to the mall or the beach, find a spot and observe how people walk. What do you learn about them from their gait? And what do you learn about yourself by watching others? Jot it all down in your journal.

Cold Laugh/Cry/Laugh

One of the more challenging cold exercises is the laugh/cry/laugh exercise. There are no prompts during this exercise. Instead, you create your own event and emotional state, eventually starting to laugh or cry and then taking that emotion as far as you can, naturally and organically, in whichever direction you start.

The purpose of this exercise is for you to have a true moment-to-moment experience, find a belief in whatever your event is and allow yourself to take that ride from the heights to the depths and back to the top again.

For example, if you start laughing, you'll crack up until you find the full story in the outburst. Let it complete itself before finding its way to the depth of your emotions where you begin to cry. At that point, you let that new part of the story take over. Finally, you'll find your way back to the moment of laughter to ride an entire loop on this emotional roller coaster.

This exercise can really get interesting if you add other people to the mix. The same instructions apply to each individual—the difference is that you are now interacting with others. This requires you to listen, trust and go with your exchange. It's a beautiful exercise that invites you to play what's in front of you, not rush it and live moment-to-moment to have a full experience, whether high or low.

Call to Action:

This exercise can be done alone or with others. Again, as you build your community, you can work together.

Cold Drunk Physical State

The cold drunk physical state exercise is probably one of the most fun exercises an actor can do, however challenging it may be.

Here is the setup: On the stage, you establish a bar, complete with a bartender, bottles of water and glasses. The teacher picks a few actors to participate. It's always good to find at least one actor who is not inhibited and is pretty good at jumping right in.

To start, the bartender pours each actor a glass of alcohol (water). The actor states the type of alcohol they're drinking, be it bourbon, tequila or wine. The teacher instructs them to drink the first glass. From there, they start to do an improv. The teacher lets the improv go for some time, then suddenly says, "Freeze." The bartender pours a second drink into each actor's glass. They consume it. The teacher tells them they are back, and they continue the improv. The actors are now two drinks in. This ritual continues through three, four and five drinks.

The challenge is for each actor to find their event in the scene, establish relationships and allow the alcohol to influence their behavior, speech and personality. Each time the teacher says "freeze," the actor advances their drunken state.

The idea of the exercise is to gradually progress from the effects of one drink to eventual inebriation. The process of this gradient *(grade, hill, incline, ramp)* helps free the actor to become more physically, emotionally, spiritually or psychologically influenced as the improvisation plays out. You'll see how relationships are established—attractions and upsets occur and people put you off or turn you on. This exercise empowers you to express yourself without inhibitions, which can be tremendously freeing. It also permits you to be a fool, misbehave and fail.

Call to Action:

This one can be a ton of fun whether you do it solo or with a group. Follow the protocol and just let it happen.

Components of the Rehearsal Process

Rehearsal

According to Dictionary.com, *rehearsal* means: "A session of exercise, drill, or practice, usually private, in preparation for a public performance, ceremony, etc."[5]

The interesting thing about most acting classes that I've attended, observed or read about, whether it be Konstantin Stanislavski, Uta Hagen, Lee Strasberg, Sanford Meisner or Stella Adler, is that while they teach people how to act, none of them seem to teach people how to rehearse.

I believe that when you give people a set of tools, you must teach them how to use them. Imagine if I gave you a gun and didn't teach you how to handle it with respect, clean it, break it down, put it back together and shoot properly. What if I didn't grill you on your reason for possessing it or instruct you on how to store the gun safely? Without hands-on knowledge of the responsibility of gun ownership, you could get in trouble, fast.

The rehearsal process provides the necessary tools to create and build a character from scratch. It teaches you how to dissect and understand the story you're telling and how to put it all together to create a work of art.

I learned the rehearsal process by observing my mentor, Milton Katselas, who invited people to watch his rehearsals. In other art forms, people have to rehearse endless hours daily to become great. A pianist has to rehearse three to six hours a day— the great ones, even more. Dancers attend class daily, and singers practice their craft just as much.

In my experience, an actor's work ethic is developed based on the artistic culture they grow up in. So, if an actor went to Juilliard or one of the performing arts schools on the East Coast, the culture was one of rolling up your sleeves and digging into the hard work. They'd have hours and hours of rehearsal, getting better and developing their singing, dancing and acting skills. The actors got used to working hard.

Actors who lack that training today often expect that their personality is enough, with some thinking they can just wing it. They tend to be lazy. A consistent rehearsal process is vital to becoming and remaining a great actor.

In this section, I'll cover the following components to help you understand how to rehearse and sharpen your skill set:

Components of the Rehearsal Process:

- Reading the material, making notes, and **Asking the Next Question**
- Honoring your genius with good-humored inflexibility
- Utilizing your **Imagination**
- Creating a Character Chart©
- 40/40/20
- Personalization ("Like the Time When I...")
- The moment before
- Improvisation
- Impinge and being impinged
- Falling in love
- Letting it go

Please note: In The Acting Lexicon (page 50), I covered several topics that are very much applicable to the rehearsal process. I will refer you back to some sections to re-read, which will help you incorporate those components into your rehearsals.

Reading the Material, Making Notes and
Asking the Next Question

The rehearsal process doesn't begin until you read the script. I will never forget when Sir Anthony Hopkins was a guest in class and had an invaluable exchange with the students.

STUDENT 1

Mr. Hopkins, what do you do after you read this script?

SIR ANTHONY HOPKINS

I read it again.

STUDENT 1

Okay, once you read it a second time, now what do you do?

SIR ANTHONY HOPKINS

I read it again.

STUDENT 2

(after a slight pause) Sir, you read the script three times! Then, what do you do?

SIR ANTHONY HOPKINS

I read it again. I read the script at least 250 times. Each time I read it, I have another idea. I take notes. I jot down all of the ideas, concepts and visions about this character. By the time I'm ready to put the script down and stand on my feet, I am so pregnant with the character that his behavior, his attitude, the way he talks, the way he thinks, is very much a part of me, and I'm ready to start realizing all the ideas I've come up with.

That makes absolute sense to me because Sir Anthony clearly allows the character to come to him. He lets the writer's words and concepts influence his thought processes in creating this person.

So, the first thing you have to do is fully understand what the writer created. You must understand why the character is in the script. What is their role in moving the story forward? Are they the protagonist, antagonist, stakes character, doubter? Each of those archetypes has a very specific job to do that will determine your approach to creating the character.

But you don't stop there. Now you embark on character development from the words and circumstances the writer has provided. The character's reality is in their history and backstory, and you discover that by **Asking the Next Question** until you are so pregnant with that character that you know exactly who this person is and where they're coming from. That's where the rehearsal process begins.

Because we live in a microwave world, which influences us to want to cook things quickly rather than slowly cook them over time for better flavor, we often feel the need to form an instant opinion about the character. Slow down—take a deeper dive into the writer's words, current circumstances and the influence their past has on them. These factors determine who this person is and how to play them best.

Begin by ***Asking the Next Question***. Like we explored in the chapter "God is in the Details" chapter (page 75), assume the writer says the character is drunk. The next question might be how drunk? What are they drinking? How much alcohol have they had? Why are they drinking? What kind of drunk are they—happy, sad or something else? As you answer those questions, you can start to fill in the blanks of the specific nature of the character.

Call to Action:

Challenge yourself to read something 250 times, adding to your notes with each reading.

After every 50 times you read it, note the difference in your knowledge, passion and interest in the story and the character.

Honoring Your Genius
with Good-Humored Inflexibility

The next component of the rehearsal process is to really understand your genius. When you begin any rehearsal process, make a commitment to yourself that you will honor your genius.

Now, let me be clear: The first order of the day is to sing the song the way it is written. In other words, really understand what the writer has given you and what they are saying.

Next, it's on you to understand the character's job in the story. What responsibility does this character have in moving the narrative forward?

Once you understand that, then you can apply your interpretation within the parameters of what the writer has given you.

Acclaimed philosopher Ralph Waldo Emerson believed your genius begins with your first impression and is supported by your "good-humored inflexibility," even "when the whole cry of voices is on the other side." Honor your viewpoint and trust the perceptions, thoughts and impulses that come to you. Don't question them. This skill is the cornerstone of your talent.

What is good-humored inflexibility? The word inflexible means not permitting change or variation, unalterable. To have good humor is to not take things personally. You have an idea, concept or point of view because it is yours, and your good humor helps you protect that viewpoint.

When working on a project, I want to give myself a chance to fail. This means I honor my vision and am not open to other people's opinions until I'm done. For example, I might say, "Thank you for wanting to make a suggestion, but right now, I would rather give my ideas a chance to fail." Or, "I appreciate your input, but for now, I would love to figure this out and allow myself to fail forward."

In other words, I give birth to the baby and let it develop before I allow other people to try to change it. All babies are ugly when they are born—that's my opinion, and I'll defend it with good-humored inflexibility. They need time to grow into themselves. When it comes to creating art, that too must go through the same process of caring and nurturing without interference from others.

So, expect your creation to be ugly at first. Be prepared to utilize **Humor, Charm and Irony** as you shape it, and let it grow into something beautiful. Insist on practicing good-humored inflexibility.

Call to Action:

Pay close attention to whether or not you allow people to change your mind about your choices, be it in life or art, and take notes. Notice how hard (or not) you fight to hold on to your belief system. Look back at how often you've done this in the past. Now, write it all down in your journal.

Utilizing Your *Imagination*

In this process of bringing your ideas to life, you are also calling upon another important component of the rehearsal process: your **Imagination**. According to Webster's Dictionary 1828:

*We would define **Imagination** to be the will working on the materials of memory, not satisfied with following the order prescribed by nature, or suggested by accident, it selects the parts of different conceptions, or objects of memory, to form a whole, more pleasing, more terrible or more awful than has ever been presented in the ordinary course of nature.*[6]

That is one helluva definition. That's almost a license to get away with murder—in the artistic sense, of course. It suggests that **Imagination** is only limited by our willingness to allow outside sources to alter our original concepts. Everything ever invented was created by someone's **Imagination**.

For example, I think about the fictional character Buck Rogers, created by Philip Francis Nowlan in 1929. It was one of the first space adventure comic strips that spawned many other comic strips, space adventure films and TV shows. Mr. Nowlan's **Imagination** had to seem preposterous to many at the time. But I'm sure that with good-humored inflexibility, he held off the naysayers.

We can see by this definition of **Imagination** that good-humored inflexibility is the permission to create in the truest sense of yourself. When you can do that, you can deter people from trying to change your creation. As Ralph Waldo Emerson said, "To be yourself in a world that is constantly trying to make you something else is the greatest accomplishment."

The rehearsal process is a way for you to honor your own opinions and ideas and give yourself a chance to fail. Failure is how you learn. Each failure provides an opportunity for another answer. Try it a new way, flip it around, turn it upside down. Utilize your *Imagination* to keep coming up with creative solutions and try things that have never been tried before, just like Mr. Nowlan did. Pull from your *Imagination* to see how far you can go. Keep going until you are absolutely convinced that you need to change your mind. That hasn't happened yet for me. But it's important that you trust in your tools, so you can try one thing, then another and another until it feels right. Creating the space for that to occur is vital.

Call to Action:

Challenge yourself to use your *Imagination* to invent or reimagine something. It doesn't matter what form it is in, be it a book idea, a short story, a better way to open a box, a new hair tie or to reinvent the wheel. Write down whatever comes to mind. Don't self-edit—trust yourself. That's the hardest part.

Creating a Character Chart©

A Character Chart© is another important component of the rehearsal process that helps you systematically study and understand who your character is.

In my early years as an actor, I worked hard to develop an understanding of my role in society. I saw how quickly art could make a difference in people's lives.

However, I have always thought it curious that when you look at a list of coveted professions, acting is way down on the list. At the top of the list are teachers, lawyers, scientists, medical professionals, IT pros and people in financial services.

It's amazing that an industry (acting) that changes the course of nature, creates whole movements, initiates changes in belief systems, gives people motivation to live and provides reflective sources like a sounding board for people to have epiphanies, can still reside at the bottom of the food chain of importance.

I've also deeply considered what I do as an artist. The guidance I received from the mentors in my life, my mother's work ethic and my ancestors' resilience have all helped me to approach my work instinctually and intentionally.

One of my teachers was an Italian opera singer named Giuseppe Balistreri. He was a voice teacher who taught until he was 95 years old. He told me, "One must master technique. At the same time, one must not be enslaved by it, for the purpose of technique is to transmit the inner meaning, the message of the text and/or music."

That quote spoke to me of structure. Structure is vital to creating anything with a beginning, middle and end. I like to think about the concept of structural functionalism when creating a Character Chart©. I know "structural functionalism" is a big concept. Understanding the various interpretations of each word gives breath and depth to its comprehension.

Structure:
1. A definite pattern of organization.

Function:
1. Taking the things you need and processing them to make the specific things you want.

So, what is structural functionalism, and how does it work?

Structural functionalism is a theory that emphasizes the importance of understanding how the parts of a system work together to produce observable behaviors. In the case of a Character Chart©, it is about understanding how each emotion the character experiences is systematically structured to work together to create a fully developed, wholly realized person. This chart helps to create a functional process of repetition, study and work ethic.

A Character Chart© is the science, or systematic study, of developing a character. Part of the chart is examining the myriad of colors and emotions that make up that character's personality. Three throughlines must be explored for character development:

Emotional Throughline: Emotional throughlines are the simple or complex emotions humans possess as part of our personality makeup. We all have a compilation of feelings: light and dark, good and bad, left and right, up and down, assets and liabilities. By examining the emotional throughlines of a character, which are both found in the script and determined by the actor, you can better understand the character.

Plot Throughline: This centers around the main events or actions of the story, the external conflict and the resolution. The plot throughline, which the writer gives you, is consistent with the emotional throughlines of a character, which the actor creates.

Theme Throughline: This explores a deeper, underlying message or idea that the piece conveys. The choices made by each character in a script should be to serve the piece's theme on one level or another.

As the script progresses, the central themes travel like a roller coaster with highs and lows and ups and downs. At some points, the hero is winning, and at other points, they are losing. As we travel through the plot points in a script, the pendulum swings back and forth between positive and negative moments, and the protagonist's emotions are affected by this precarious roller coaster ride. Hence, the three throughlines (plot, theme and emotional) are all in tandem.

Using myself as an example to better illustrate emotional throughlines, let's examine my assets and liabilities. Assets are the lighter qualities I possess as a human being, and liabilities are the darker qualities (see page 277 for details). If we consider my assets, you will find that I am kind, thoughtful, generous, loving, passionate, understanding, supportive and empathetic. If we look at some of my liabilities, you will find I am selfish, rageful, jealous, revengeful, short-tempered and have no filter. These qualities weave in and out of my life, not unlike the colors in a Persian rug. The color red is not always dominant in the carpet. Sometimes it is front and center. Other times, it's in the background. The character is the same way. They possess qualities that will show up at one time or another, in different degrees of intensity.

For instance, when you look at the emotional throughlines of a character in a script, you might discover that this person grapples with anger. But they don't express it at the same level from page one to page 100—there are different degrees throughout the script. When you consider the progression of the character throughout the story, you may find that anger is present in seven scenes. Each scene has a different degree, ranging from mildly pissed off to violent rage, escalating as the climax of the story nears.

In Jeffrey Alan Schechter's wonderful book about story structure, *My Story Can Beat Up Your Story*, he mentions that in every good movie, the protagonist travels through four archetypal stages of growth to reach resolution. These stages are called orphan, wanderer, warrior and martyr.[7] If we're talking about just anger alone, the level of rage during the orphan stage of the character will be different than that of the warrior stage. The same is true for any other emotion that may be a part of this character's journey. These emotional components are a part of their life, and they weave in and out throughout the story.

By creating a Character Chart©, you can map who this person is by noting when and how their emotional throughlines weave in and out throughout the script. As a result, you can pinpoint what is happening emotionally with the character, and to what degree, from one scene to the next.

Call to Action:

Create a spreadsheet. Choose one of your favorite films and pick a character you want to assess. Write down each emotion the character exhibits in each line of the script—anger, sadness, happiness, jealousy, humor, charm, irony, silliness, etc. Each time the character displays one of those emotions denotes the degree of emotion that is expressed on a scale of 1-10.

40/40/20

It's important to use time effectively in the rehearsal process. I've created a concept called *40/40/20* to guide actors in this critical endeavor.

For example, say you have a month to work on a character. Divide the time into three segments:

- Part I: Intake (40 percent; approximately 12 days): Research and gather information, read the script repeatedly to harvest ideas that come to you and **Ask the Next Question.**

- Part II: Output (40 percent; approximately 12 days): Apply the information you've harvested to the character and to other aspects of the rehearsal process (i.e., does your character have an accent? Walk with a limp? Have uncontrollable rage?).

- Part III: Lock it in (20 percent; approximately 6 days): Solidify what you've learned; don't try to change anything at the last minute. At this point, you're operating out of abundance and not scarcity. You're locking in your product and trying to get into a place where you absolutely believe in what you're doing.

Using the 40/40/20 concept, you can maximize your time during the rehearsal process to create a fully formed character, because when you **Do Your Best, You Can Forget the Rest.**

You can move on to the next thing without carrying the fear of failure with you.

Call to Action:

Incorporate strategic time management into your daily tasks so you can learn how to maximize your results. The next time you cook a meal, clean the house, do your taxes or paint a room, apply this methodology to your process. Make it a point to *Do Your Best and Forget the Rest.*

Personalization
("Like the Time When I...")

Personal:
1. Of or relating to what is true and authentic for you.

In the chapter, "What's the Real Truth?" (page 108), I included a quote by the acting teacher Konstantin Stanislavski. I wanted to share it again as a reminder to be personal in your work:

"Never be afraid of an author. An actor is a free artist. You want to create an image that is different from the author's. When the two images—the author's and the actor's—fuse into one, then a true artistic work is created."

Everything you do in art should come from within. As you start working on certain aspects of the script during the rehearsal process, you want to make it personal. How do you do that—especially when you've never experienced something the character has?

First, as I've pointed out, what you give to a character will always be an extension of your life to some degree. As you look at a character and **Ask the Next Question** at a particular moment in a script, you can apply the concept "like the time when I…"

For example, if there is a certain emotion that you think is called for in your character, you can know that intellectually, but you must also be able to act and experience the emotion on a visceral level. So, make it personal:

"Yeah, that feeling of rage that the writer expresses about my character was like the time when my cat got killed by three coyotes."

Side note: This really happened to me! I remember it so vividly because I was awakened at 3 am by a loud screech and the bark and growl of not one...not two...but three separate coyotes. I jumped out of bed when I realized it was my cat, Georgie. I ran to the window, only to see one coyote grabbing Georgie by the back of his neck, another tearing his stomach in half while the third coyote was moving in to finish him off. It was utterly devastating. Remembering your emotional state is one way to make something personal.

The other and more important part is identifying the *behavior* associated with that incident. Was my hand shaking? Was my heart beating so fast that I couldn't speak? Did I stutter? Was I wiping the sweat off my face? If I remember the behavior associated with that particular moment of rage and apply it during the rehearsal process, it becomes an essential part of the creation of my character.

Remember, your emotions are tied to muscle memory. Specific behavior will elicit specific emotions.

Making emotional connections means your work becomes more personal, connected, visceral and specific. You won't be playing some surface, unrealized level of rage, heartbreak or love. Instead, you'll be having an authentic experience that is connected to moments and behavior from your own life.

That's being personal. That's bringing you to the part. And the more personal you are in your acting work, the more of an experience you and the audience will have.

Call to Action:

Recall a dramatic incident—a funeral, a wedding or an argument. Try to remember the moment as vividly as possible. How did you act? Do you remember what your hands were doing? Was your heart beating fast? Did your voice quiver? Now, try to duplicate that behavior to see what feelings come up. Record your observations in your journal.

The Moment Before

Refer to the chapter "The Moment Before" on page 59.

Improvisation

Improvisation is being given an unknown or known set of circumstances without a script. It's an unscripted reality, experience and exchange by one or more people that creates a story in an immediate moment.

In the rehearsal process, improvisation can be a valuable tool to fill in needed information about the character that isn't clear or specific in the script. When the writing is good, there will be clues about what is missing. Improvisation is a tool that can help with backstory about a relationship or the history of a conflict. For instance, if two brothers are hostile towards each other, it would be helpful to know how this conflict started. Maybe when they were 16, their dad gave one kid the keys to his prized Corvette and the other kid nothing. That could be the source of envy or rage. Or maybe the kid who got the car immediately handed the keys to his brother, and we learn how much they loved each other. Both scenarios would give us information that could help us determine the brothers' current motivations.

Improvisation is a wonderful tool for discovering things not necessarily written in the script, and freeing us from fixed ideas and preconceived notions about a character.

Call to Action:

Give yourself the challenge of making something up as you go along. Whether it's fixing dinner, deciding to take a different route somewhere or going into a store having no idea what you want to buy. Make the event an improvisation.

Impinge and Being Impinged

Impinge:

1. Make an impact on, make an impression on, strike against, hit, impact.

Acting is about being affected, feeling something and having an experience. So, if you're acting with somebody, your ideas, concepts and feelings need to strike against them to make them uncomfortable, to make them think, to make them feel an emotion and to help create conflict and contradiction in their character.

Likewise, if someone impinges on you with a feeling, thought, idea, dialogue or action, you have to react to it—but not until you receive it and it moves you somehow.

This is a critical point, so let me reiterate: To be impinged, you must allow whatever you receive from your fellow actor to truly land. This helps you determine how to respond or impinge your fellow actor, and to what degree. You must be intentional in what you send to them. Your communication with them—both verbal and non-verbal—has an impact.

Art is meant to make an impression. It should make a person feel something, be it the scene partner or the audience. Sometimes its effect is real, palpable and immediate. Others, it may take a moment before it really gets through you (see "Reflective Delay," page 86). We often see this on the 6 o'clock news, when reporters stick a microphone in someone's face when they've just witnessed a tragedy. That person must describe something that hasn't fully hit them yet.

If you are acting on a surface level, not truly digging in and allowing yourself to be vulnerable, then you aren't impinging on anyone. If you and your scene partner have all your lines memorized but are mechanically going through the motions without intention or understanding, you are not impinging on each other. Your performance becomes a rote, back-and-forth exchange of your lines.

When you say "hello" to someone, and you mean it, there is energy. It is an acknowledgment. And the response from the other person reflects that energy exchange.

This type of energy exchange also has to exist in your acting work. Art must have a strong degree of impingement. You impinge by striking forward, and you also impinge by drawing away—meaning that you make a concerted effort to *not* communicate or engage. That withdrawal is also an impingement, because it affects both you and your scene partner.

Without impingement, you are creating a milquetoast character. Merriam-Webster defines a milquetoast as "a timid, meek, or unassertive person."[8] An unassertive person with an unassertive communication style does not land or penetrate. Therefore, their art is milquetoast in nature.

Call to Action:

As you go through your daily life, pay attention to exchanges you have with other people where you are affected by what they say or do. Also, pay attention to how you affect others by addressing or reacting to them. Take notes in your journal.

Falling in Love

When a script calls for two characters to fall in love, there has to be a believable connection between you and your scene partner. The training and application of this component in the rehearsal process is important because you may be acting with someone you don't know. If you've never worked with a person before, you have to find a way to connect quickly on an intimate and meaningful level because, in film and TV, you are rarely afforded the luxury of lengthy rehearsal. You meet your co-star on the day of shooting and only have a few minutes to connect with them before the director yells, "Action!"

So, your first job as an actor is to fall in love with your fellow artist. It allows you to be present, open and available to what's in front of you. It also allows for trust. By falling in love, you will have more permission to "just be," so that you can be impinged and have a moment-to-moment experience with your scene partner.

I don't care if the person you're acting with is the antagonist or the protagonist in the story. There must be chemistry between you and the person you're acting with so your relationship translates on screen or stage. The connection has to be believable, whether it's a young high school couple, a husband and wife, a mother and daughter, best friends, friendly coworkers or ex-lovers who still have feelings for each other. Falling in love is one of the first orders of the day.

The first step to falling in love is to be present. The willingness to see and be seen—to really take in the person in front of you. What color are their eyes? How are their eyebrows shaped? Do they have long lashes? Look at the shape of their nose. Do they have full lips? High cheekbones, maybe? A round face? Long face? How white are their teeth? Do they have little or big ears? What color is their hair? Is it long or short?

Falling in love also requires you to be a good listener. If you can listen, you can respond. Acting is a back-and-forth exchange. It's not sending something out and letting the recipient do whatever they want with it. It's a tennis match. If you're playing tennis, you can't hit the lob unless you wait for it to come down. Decide where you're going to place it.

The exchange between yourself and the actor you're playing with is important. If you're listening, that exchange can happen. If you take the actor's hand, you can feel their energy and want them to feel yours. This takes being open and vulnerable. You want them to feel confident and safe. If you hug them, you want them to feel the sincerity in your hug. You also want to receive the energy they are sharing.

After the initial "getting to know you" period, you may want to try an intimacy exercise with your scene partner during the rehearsal process:

- Start by standing face-to-face at slightly less than an arm's distance apart, and hold each other's hands while you look at each other.
- As you become more and more comfortable, close the distance.
- Now, each person shares what they observe about the other person.
- Allow the distance to progress gently to a full-on hug.

- As you're in the hug, you can share how you feel with each new gradient, whether there is an increase in comfort or discomfort, and then adjust accordingly.
- If true, you can also address how good it makes you feel.
- You may want to create a safety signal that lets you out of the exercise if you feel uncomfortable. Consent is an important aspect of any intimacy exercise.

Additions to this exercise include:

- Dancing together, fast or slow.
- Sitting next to each other on the couch and, with permission, touching each other's face, arm or leg.
- Laying down on the couch or bed and snuggling (only after establishing boundaries).

Call to Action:

This is a good one. As you communicate with others, try to be intentional about how you exchange with them. Be present and willing to give and receive. Don't bail because you may feel uncomfortable or if you perceive they may feel uncomfortable. Work through it. You may fall in love.

Letting It Go

In life, there are no pre-written scripts. If you say, "I'm gonna go to Neiman Marcus and buy some clothes," nobody hands you a script that details the trip. You can only live moment-to-moment. The conversation with the person at the checkout counter is organic. The dialogue happens as you live it.

The thing with art is that, yes, you play a character. Yes, you learn the lines. Yes, you do the anthropological work. Yes, you create a Character Chart©. Yes, you learn everything about the person you're playing. Then, you have to *let it go*.

You must trust that what you've learned about the character is in your DNA. You know all that's necessary, and you don't have to think. You cannot predetermine the nuances of how it's going to go. You have to live in the moment and let it happen. Otherwise, your interaction could come across as forced, phony and pretentious. It might sound predictable and planned, and the audience can see your performance's blueprint.

This rehearsal component goes hand-in-hand with 40/40/20. You've gone through the whole preparation process, and then you let it go. Again, with 40/40/20, the first 40 percent—intake—is about receiving information, research and data and learning as much as possible about what the writer has given you. The next 40 percent—output—is about implementing what you gathered during the intake process. And the last 20 percent is ultimately the process of letting it go. Now that you've gotten all of this information in your mind, body, system, heart and DNA, it is time for you to trust your performance.

These are the components of the rehearsal process. If you understand and apply these components, you'll have a substantive rehearsal process. The knowledge of the character you gain at this point makes a tremendous difference in the story you tell, the lives you change and the people you affect, starting with the actor you're working with.

One final thing I'll say: The rehearsal process does not require agreement (with the exception of intimacy exercises). You're not looking for someone to agree with your interpretation. You're not trying to get on the same page with somebody else because life is not like that. You meet people on the street you've never seen before, and they respond to you in a way that sometimes you didn't expect. You have to be open to the process.

I was doing a play called *Ma Rainey's Black Bottom* by August Wilson. I played Levee, a trumpeter, with the hots for Ma Rainey's girlfriend, Bessie Mae.

One day, Bessie comes down into the band room to flirt with Levee. She sits down on this long bench, and they begin to chat. He has one foot on the bench, trumpet in hand, and he leans down and starts talking to her in a low, seductive voice. Bessie is very interested in what Levee has to say. He straddles the bench facing her and reaches to touch her beautiful, brown, exposed thigh.

During the rehearsal, as soon as I touched her thigh, the actress playing Bessie stopped the scene.

ACTRESS

Please don't touch my leg.

RICHARD

Why not?

ACTRESS

Because I don't like people touching me.

RICHARD

Oh…okay. I understand that.

Richard looks at her for a moment before continuing.

RICHARD

Well… Richard completely understands that, but Levee, on the other hand, is going to touch that leg. That's a beautiful leg. He would not pass up that opportunity. If you don't want Levee to touch Bessie Mae's leg, then Bessie is going to have to move because Levee is definitely going to try to touch that leg because you and I both know this scene ends in a passionate kiss. Let's rehearse.

The actress went back to the door and re-entered the room as Bessie, and the scene proceeded just as it had earlier. Bessie straddled the bench, and Levee also straddled the bench facing her. Levee reached out to touch her thigh, and Bessie slid back a few inches. Levee moved forward a few inches and tried to feel that thigh again. Bessie scooted further down the bench, and Levee followed suit. The scene became this wonderful cat and mouse game that proved to be extremely seductive and sexy.

Finally, Levee walked Bessie to the end of the bench. She stood up, and he slowly backed her against the door, where he finally kissed her. It was a remarkable, unforgettable moment. If I had gone into agreement with the actress, that moment would've never been as powerful as it was.

Woodie King Jr., the most prolific producer of Black literature in this country's history, saw that production and told me that he produced two plays that tried to duplicate that moment.

Call to Action:

Letting it go is all about trusting yourself. The next time you have an opportunity to speak, sing, dance or confront an important topic, summon up the courage to embrace the moment and trust that you will do it successfully.

Components
of an Audition

The audition process should be fun, like putting together a puzzle. It's taking all the tools you have learned and applying them to solve it.

You must understand that no two puzzles are alike, so you can go forth knowing there is no competition. You are not competing with anyone except yourself and your ability to **Do Your Best and Forget the Rest**.

The audition process doesn't have to be a mystery. Once you know the various components, you can master the process, thereby avoiding going in and just hoping for the best.

Understanding the components puts you in the driver's seat because you have gained certainty and confidence. It can, at the very least, help you book the room.

"Booking the room" is a concept I teach my students to focus on, because that is one element of the process you actually have control over. So many variables go into casting, but delivering a solid, professional product with a great attitude ensures that the people in the room become your fans and will bring you back for other opportunities. That is what booking the room means.

Having been in the business since 1969, I have attended thousands of auditions. As a result of this collective knowledge, I created the components of an audition to help you understand everything that needs to occur on both a technical and performance level from the moment you receive an audition to the moment you leave the audition room or turn in that self-tape.

With a thorough understanding and application of these components, you will operate like a professional and "book the room" every single time.

The components of an audition support the larger picture. Think of it like choreography. Choreography is a series of dance steps that support the larger picture of a dance piece. You learn each dance one step at a time. Each step builds upon the next to tell a story. And the more you rehearse those moves, the more fluid and cohesive they become. Eventually, you'll arrive at a place where you are no longer thinking about the steps. They are now living inside of you, and those steps form a complete, fully realized dance.

Similarly, when you master the components of an audition, you will move seamlessly from one component to the next, creating a complete audition experience from start to finish.

In this section, I will describe the Components of an Audition on both a technical and performance level so that you can understand the bigger picture. The following is an overview:

Technical Components:

- o Entering the room
- *Life Force*
- The definition of "audition"
- It's your living room
- Controlling the room
    - Setting the place of the reader
    - Sitting versus standing: comfortability or storytelling
    - Holding script at the four o'clock position to set the frame of the camera
    - Marking of the script

- Finding spotting points for the other characters in the scene
- Slating
- Playing within the frame

Performance Components:

- Fulfilling the causative routine
- Postulating the results
○ Handling the waiting room
- ***Claiming for Oneself***
- Taking a moment
- Breathing
- Letting go of vanity
- Having a moment before
- You should be completely off-book
- Impinge and be impinged
- Allowing the scene to occur, have patience and don't get on a train
- Don't flinch and deliver your product
- Finishing the scene
- Recapturing and exiting the room
- Performing a ceremony of respect

○ = Applies to in-person auditions only.
● = Applies to in-person, self-tape and virtual auditions.

Technical Components of an Audition

Entering the Room

Why is this component listed first? Because first impressions are everything. They happen instantly. Either the people in the room like you or they don't. Either they want to get to know you, or they don't.

Before you walk into the room, the needle is at zero—it's a level playing field. The people in the room have not formed an opinion of you yet. When you enter with a particular attitude or energy, the needle either goes into the green zone, which indicates that they like you and are interested in you, or it goes into the red, which indicates that they don't.

How do you make the needle go into the green? By entering the room with **Life Force**.

Life:
1. A source of animating energy.

Force:
1. Impact and impetus.

How do you harness your **Life Force?** Your **Life Force** is connected to and influenced by your raison d'être, or reason for being. When you understand that, you are alive. You carry yourself with vitality, confidence and buoyancy. You have a force that is present, and running like an engine.

When you walk into a room with **Life Force**, the molecules in the room change, and people sit up, lean in and become interested. They like you and feel at ease with you.

The same applies to self-tape auditions or live virtual auditions. In a self-tape, the only opportunity casting has to get a glimpse of your personality is in your slate. (We will get to that component just a little later). Your slate needs to be infused with your **Life Force**, so that casting immediately receives a sense of who you are.

In a live virtual audition, you will be on camera and most likely in a close-up. If your **Life Force** is present, they will see your confidence, certainty and undeniable presence. They will notice that you're **On Go**, making strong choices and controlling the room. Conversely, if you're lacking **Life Force**, the people in the room will see your nerves, insecurities, shyness or negative energy. This can cost you the audition before you even get to act in the room.

The Definition of "Audition"

From the American Heritage Dictionary:
> *1. A trial performance by an actor, dancer or musician to demonstrate suitability or skill.*
> *2. The sense or power of hearing.*[9]

I am most interested in the second definition: the sense or power of hearing. This empowers you to actively be present and engaged as soon as you enter the room. You will be attuned to everything happening in front of you. You will be able to take everyone in, know how many people are in the room, what they are wearing and what they are saying to you. When they greet you and ask you questions, you can respond in a connected, genuine way. All of this sets you up to be in a better place to deliver your product. The sense or power of hearing also applies to live virtual auditions.

Most actors understand the definition of an audition as a trial performance, as by an actor, dancer or musician, to demonstrate suitability or skill. And the keyword they latch onto is *trial*.

Have you ever felt that you were being put on trial at an audition? Did you develop this sense of fear and dread? "Oh God! They are going to judge me. They are going to judge my skills as an actor."

They, they, they. This ominous, judgmental "they" that you create makes it feel like a trial. That's the mindset you must overcome when approaching an audition.

It's Your Living Room

When you are home, you have a sense of comfort and familiarity. You are not self-conscious and rigid as you live in your space. If I came to your house, you would be warm and inviting. You would ask me what I want to eat or drink and encourage me to make myself comfortable.

Be just as relaxed and easy when you are in the audition room.

"Hey, how's it going? It's great to be here."
"I love your shoes. Where'd you get them?"
"I love your shirt. That's a great color on you."

The audition room is your living room, and the people in the room are your guests. You must make them feel comfortable because it's your place and it's your time.

Ultimately, it's your job to lose. This same component applies to live virtual auditions. Be welcoming and easygoing in that space as well.

Controlling the Room

There's a famous expression that goes, "Ask, and you shall receive." Or, as my friend Dana Pump likes to say, "If you don't ask, you don't get."

Controlling the room means asking for things you need to deliver your product in the best light possible. Typically, your audition is sent later to the people who ultimately make the casting decisions. Occasionally, these decision-makers are watching you live from another room or location. Controlling the room sets you up to shine in front of these decision-makers, regardless of when they see your audition.

Ask for what you need to ace your audition with *Humor, Charm and Irony*; don't be shy. What's the worst that could happen? They say no? Okay, if they say no, it's all good. You have prepared your product beforehand and can still deliver it successfully.

Setting the Place of the Reader

This is your opportunity to get what you need from the person you'll be acting with. With *Humor, Charm and Irony,* you can ask them to stand closer to the camera for eyeline purposes. This way, you avoid acting in profile. You may also ask them to sit or stand, depending on the circumstances of the scene. If your scene partner has the first line, you can tell them you will give them a signal off-frame so they know when to say it. Otherwise, they may jump in too quickly with their first line and throw you off.

Sitting versus Standing: Comfortability or Storytelling

Do you sit in the audition because it makes you feel more comfortable and present, or do you sit because it's part of the storytelling? Similarly, do you stand because it makes you feel more comfortable and present, or do you stand because it's part of the storytelling? You should decide based on what will best serve you and the story.

Holding Script at the Four O'Clock Position to Set the Frame of the Camera

Here's a surefire way to ensure you never break the relationship with the reader when you're auditioning: hold the script at four o'clock.

Why does this work? Because if you're in the middle of an exchange with the reader and need your next line, only your eyes will look down. That way, on camera, it doesn't look like you are reading. Without this subtle positioning, you'll look to the side or down with your entire head to get the next line, breaking the relationship with the reader and the viewer.

To hold the script at four o'clock, follow these instructions:

- Hold your sides straight out in front of you.
- Visualize the numbers on a clock, with 12 o'clock straight above you and three o'clock directly in front of you.
- Now, move the script to the four o'clock position.
- Finally, ask whoever is filming you to frame you in a close-up: "Excuse me? Would you mind zooming in and

framing me right above my sides so I'm in a close-up? Thank you so much."

Marking of the Script

With your script in the four o'clock position, look over the top of the script and observe what you see. Since you are standing in front of the camera, it may be part of the tripod or the top of a chair. Use whatever you see to mark that spot as where your script should be held.

Find Spotting Points for the Other Characters in the Scene

If there's only one other character in the scene, you can assign that character to the reader and act with them.

However, if you're dealing with multiple characters, the reader will only be one of the characters, so you must find points in the room to represent the other characters in the scene.

When you're in the audition room, find something specific to look at—a nail or a small dark mark on the wall so your eyes focus on each "character" (point) in a sharp, laser-like way. Otherwise, your eyes will look glassy with nothing specific to focus on.

You can also create the illusion that you're speaking to multiple characters in a self-tape or live virtual audition with a variation of this technique. Take a Super Sticky Post-it® Note, draw a dot in the middle of it, and place it behind the camera on your wall. Repeat the same process for the other characters, remembering that the reader will be one of the characters.

Even though you're playing against dots on the wall, you don't have to worry about your performance. You've done the work beforehand to carve out all of the characters so that you won't be acting in a robotic, general way with these points. Instead, your acting will be visceral, alive and specific.

Slating

A slate is your opportunity to introduce yourself on camera to the decision-makers who will watch your audition. It is the first thing they see when they play your audition. It's the first time—and sometimes the only time—they get a sense of who you are. Think about how you say hello to your friends. It's easy, comfortable and full of *Life Force*. Apply that approach to your slates.

Playing Within the Frame

In film, the frame is your stage, and playing within it allows you to create a reality and life to tell a particular story. How do you play within the frame during your audition?

Let's look at some examples. If you're greeting another character in the scene, do you extend your hand off-frame to shake their hand? Do you convey in your acting how that handshake impinges you? If the scene takes place in a library, do you reach off-frame to grab a book? And do you examine it off-frame before putting it back on the shelf? Even though you're not really shaking someone's hand or taking an actual book off the shelf, the behavior creates a reality for the viewer. You conjure a specific reality off-frame that your audience buys into because they fill it in with their **Imagination**.

Do you walk into the frame when you start the scene because you're coming from somewhere and have exciting or urgent news to share? Do you pop your head into frame as if you were peeking into your boss's office to say, "Hey, boss—you got a second?" "Sure, come on in." And then you bring your whole body into frame to proceed with the scene? The story is always paramount. Never use the frame arbitrarily. Doing so will only distract from the story and make you seem like you're trying too hard to be interesting or clever.

***

These are the technical components of an audition.

You may be thinking to yourself, "Wow! That's a lot. And that's just the *technical* components. Doing all of them will take up so much time in the audition room." Not at all.

Once you understand the technical and performance components like the back of your hand, you will move seamlessly from one to the next. Again, it's like choreography. The audition dance will become second nature to you.

Performance Components of an Audition

Fulfilling the Causative Routine

Causative:
1. To bring something about.

Routine:
1. To create a familiar habit.

Do you have a daily routine? For example, a makeup regimen? Or a workout routine? Whatever it is, it's safe to say that it rarely changes. It flows naturally from A to B to C, like a ritual.

We are creatures of habit, and much of our lives are routine. Most people adopt a specific routine because it provides the benefit of comfort or familiarity. A student once told me about her makeup routine, and when I asked why she does it and how it makes her feel, she replied it makes her feel feminine and womanly. Another student shared that her workout routine makes her feel healthier and clears her head in the morning. It sets her up for the day and allows her creativity to flourish because her blood is pumping.

If I were to have a camera on you for 24 hours, I would discover your routine. I would see the specific order that you do things in the morning. I would see the route you take to and from work every day. I would see the things you do when you come home from work or school. All of us have a routine—some positive, some negative. Negative routines don't serve us and are not healthy for us. We typically adopt them to avoid confronting something in our lives.

Examine your routine for an audition. I have seen many actors develop negative routines, typically tied to past auditioning experiences. The actor may procrastinate when they receive an audition and wait until the last minute to work on it. They become intimidated when they look at the number of sides, the size of the role or the genre of the material. They don't ask anyone for help with their audition. They party the night before and eat the wrong foods on audition day. Or, they don't eat anything at all, so they lack the energy to act or even be present in the audition room. Does any of this sound familiar? If you have a negative routine that you consistently repeat, you will find yourself confronting the same narrative that you always hear from **K-SHIT FM**.

I want to empower you to adopt a routine that puts you in the driver's seat and helps you be the best you can be. I've created a process known as the causative routine that will allow you to do just that. It's a step-by-step approach to tackling the audition process with clarity, confidence and professionalism from beginning to end. It also helps you identify what doesn't serve you and teaches you how to replace those negative habits with positive actions. Moving forward, I encourage you to adopt the causative routine below and make this an integral part of your audition process.

- When you get an audition, don't decide whether you like the role. Just decide to have fun with the process.

- Research the project, producers, directors and casting directors who will be in the room. Learn about the buyers you are selling to with a simple Google or IMDb search.
- Make a commitment to yourself and a buddy (someone who supports you) that you will not question your choices and ideas.
- Promise to write down all the choices and ideas that come to you.
- Do all six steps of the Subtees Process (this is explained in greater detail in the next chapter, page 205).

  - Read your sides, character's history and subtext out loud at least 15 times, or until you have that "a-ha" moment.
  - Read your sides, character's history and subtext out loud with a partner at least five times.
  - Read your sides, character's history and subtext out loud from memory with the same partner at least five times.
  - Now, act the part at least five times with your partner.
  - Switch roles with your partner and have them act your part at least five times.
  - Switch back and put yourself on camera to see if your work is clearly translating on screen.

- After you have prepared the part, you can now decide to go or not to go (they are both empowering). Just don't ride the fence.
- Make a list of estimable actions that support your game and do them.

- Make a list of the acts that lessen your esteem and commit to not doing them until this game is over.
- Handle one person, place or thing before you go to the audition. (To handle someone is to have a confrontation with them in which you take back the power that you gave them).
- Commit to taking the character public. Taking the character public is when you dress in the character's wardrobe, go out in public and exist as that character. For example, if I'm playing a character that has been drinking and has had one too many, I go to a bar and fully commit to playing that part so that others believe that I am that drunk.
- Arrive early.
- Take someone with you to the audition until you feel confident about this kind of game.
- Commit to staying the course with your choices to the very end.
- Embrace failure.
- Leave it in the room.
- Perform a ceremony of respect afterward.

Postulating the Results

Simply put, a postulate is a prediction. As it relates to the performance components of an audition, it's all about where you're looking. When you prepare for an audition, are you looking at everything that will go right? Or are you looking at everything that will go wrong?

Both options are valid because you manifest what you focus on. Visualize how you want everything to go right. "I am realizing this character to the best of my ability. I am going to make this character personal and marry myself to them. I am going to have a lot of fun exploring this scene from moment-to-moment. On audition day, I will eat a healthy breakfast that energizes me. I will play empowering music in my car on the way to the audition. I am going to arrive early and find a great parking spot. I am going to walk inside the casting office and sign in confidently. The casting assistant and I will exchange warm, friendly smiles as I finish signing in. I will sit in the waiting room and be relaxed and present..."

Postulate the results to put yourself in the zone of delivering a good, solid performance.

Handling the Waiting Room

You might be thinking to yourself, "Wait a minute. Why is this included in the Performance Components of an Audition? How does this affect my performance?"

It has everything to do with performance because many things in the waiting room can throw you off or distract you. For example, actors who loudly show off their list of credits and recent bookings. Actors who want to talk your head off before you walk into the casting director's office. Actors who get in your head and make you start questioning your choices. Actors who size you up and look you up and down, their subtext filled with critique and judgment.

All of this can lead to you comparing yourself to other actors in the room and feeling you do not belong there. If you allow others to hijack your attention, you will be thrown off your A-game because you are not fully present.

So, handle the waiting room as needed. Do not let people distract or intimidate you. Stop second-guessing yourself. Do what you need to stay present and focused on the product you are about to deliver. Wait in the hallway if that helps. Put on music if that re-focuses you. Tell the chatty person that you will speak to them after your audition.

Claiming for Oneself

When you have done the work and have turned over every stone in preparing for your part, you have earned a level of certainty. Having certainty means that you have answered all of the questions that you had when you first started working on the part. You can now, with pride, claim it for yourself. You know that you can deliver the product that you created without any doubt. *You Have Done Your Best, So You Can Now Forget the Rest*. It is now your job to lose.

Taking a Moment

Take a moment before you start the audition to get centered and present. Close your eyes, take a breath or clear your throat—whatever you need to get into the zone and ready to act.

Now, the key word here is "moment." Don't take a long time to get focused. The casting directors are on a tight schedule, so keep it moving. Also, don't use taking a moment as an opportunity to do things that may paint you as unprofessional or amateur. Don't start doing yoga poses, jumping jacks or vocal exercises. It's a quick moment that grounds you for your performance.

Breathing

Breathing helps you stay present and grounded. It connects to your emotions, voice and point of view. Don't get so tight that you prevent yourself from feeling and having an experience during your performance.

Letting Go of Vanity

Vanity:
1. Being self-absorbed in your own appearance and imperfections.

Your job is to serve the story and the character. You must leave your vanity at the door when you create art. You can't be concerned about how you look or are being perceived. Vanity doesn't allow you to embody a character that resonates and impinges.

If you take excessive pride in your appearance, qualities and abilities, you forget about playing the truth of the character. Not every character requires full-on makeup or needs to be impeccably dressed. Not every character needs to look "perfect." These things serve your vanity and your ego.

Get out of the way and discover what you need to let go of to play a character. Otherwise, the characters you play will always be hollow, worthless, pointless and empty. Be "ugly" for the character and lend your perceived "flaws" to them.

Vanity also affects your breathing, because if you are self-conscious about letting your belly hang out, you will be sucking in your gut and cutting off your breath throughout your audition. You can't act if you're not breathing. You can't feel and experience, let alone speak. Release the gut. Breathe and connect to the character's point of view.

Having a Moment Before

As we've discussed (page 59), the moment before is the most critical in a scene because it contains all the data that allows you to enter a scene with the appropriate amount of energy, emotion and intention. It sets the tone and trajectory of the scene. The reality of the moment before can only be determined by the event of the scene.

When you know what the scene you're auditioning with is about, you can shape a clear moment before that supports the event, and helps you start the scene on the right path. It dictates your behavior and your psychological and physical states. It fuels the life and experience of your character before the scene begins.

When you enter the stage or enter the frame of the camera, the viewer should feel a life that is continuing. You should already be in belief with the event of the scene as you enter.

However, most actors don't do that. They come on and *then* start acting the scene. There isn't that initial plié—that important launch—into the scene. They start the scene on the first line, but the scene never starts on the first line. There is a specific life and experience that needs to occur before the first line of the scene is even spoken.

You Should Be Completely Off-Book

Why? When you are tied to the script, you cut off the circular exchange (a fluid exchange where the actor is not looking away to get the next line) and the connection between you and your reader. You cut off creative possibilities. However, you should always have your script with you and hold it at four o'clock just in case you forget a line. It's always there, so the flow is never broken.

When you're off-book, you're connected and present. You play and act better with your reader because you've created an opportunity to impinge and be impinged.

Impinge and Be Impinged

Acting is about being affected, feeling something and having an experience. If you're acting with somebody, your ideas, concepts and feelings need to strike against them to make them uncomfortable, to make them think, to make them feel an emotion, to create conflict and contradiction in their character, etc. Likewise, if someone impinges on you with a feeling, thought, idea, dialogue or action, you have to react to it. You can't go forth with the next response until you receive it and it moves you in some way. That's very important.

To be impinged, you must allow whatever you receive from your fellow actor to truly land. To impinge your fellow actor, you need to be intentional in what you send out to them. Your communication (both verbal and non-verbal) has to make an impact. If you act on a surface level, where you are not truly digging in and not allowing yourself to be vulnerable, then you're not impinging each other. If you're working with another actor in a scene, it's not enough to have your lines memorized. If you're mechanically going through the motions and not truly having an intention with what you're saying or understanding what the other person is saying, then you are not impinging on each other.

Allow the Scene to Occur,
Have Patience and Don't Get On a Train

Don't let your nerves get the best of you. You'll rush, miss moments and act mechanically. If you do, the next thing you know, the audition is over, and you have no idea what just happened or how it went.

Don't Flinch and Deliver Your Product

According to Dictionary.com, *flinch* means: "To draw back or shrink, as from what is dangerous, difficult, or unpleasant."[10]

You put so much time and work into creating a product from your **Imagination** and impulses. You made a personal connection to the scene and carved out a specific character. Deliver your product as planned.

Some actors will flinch and change their product in the waiting room. They start comparing themselves to the other actors. They think that they aren't enough. This can happen to you, too. You come in dressed differently from everyone else in the room, and suddenly, you want to conform and assimilate to fit in. You hear another actor auditioning in the room, and the casting director is laughing hysterically, so you begin to second-guess yourself.

Don't flinch and change your product in the audition itself. If the people in the room aren't responding how you thought they would, don't try to be interesting or work harder in your performance. Avoid letting anxiety change your product. Resist the pressure to be "perfect" or "right." Don't try to figure out what the casting directors want. Stay the course and deliver your product. Let them know that this is how the character goes. You could very well be the answer they are looking for. Otherwise, you will deliver a watered-down, derivative version of what you intended.

Finish the Scene

Just like the scene doesn't start on the first line, it also doesn't end on the last line. There is still a life occurring after the last line of every scene. What is the character thinking? How are they responding and dealing with the information they've received? How are they processing what just occurred after the other character leaves, and they are now alone in the privacy of their thoughts?

When you end the scene right after the last line, it's a jarring experience for the viewers. It feels like you slammed on the breaks and cut the experience short.

Letting the scene end creates a beautiful button for the journey you took the viewer on. A sense of completion and finality occurs. A prominent casting director once told me that directors look for actors who know how to let the scene end because they love to see how they continue living as the character even after the last line is spoken.

There is gold in those final moments.

Recapturing and Exiting the Room

Once the scene ends, recapture the room as yourself: "Thank you. I appreciate the opportunity."

This simple cap creates a powerful sense of finality in the audition room because you did a great job in your performance, and now you're reminding the viewer again about what a great person you are. This leaves them wanting more from you. It creates a sense of loss and longing after you leave the room. "Wow, not only was she a good actor, but she was also nice, friendly and professional."

Once you recapture the room, leave. Don't linger. Don't try to make awkward small talk that may diminish any positive impact you made. The only exception is if the people in the room want to chat with you or give you a re-direct. Be sure to exit with the same *Life Force* you entered with.

Perform a Ceremony of Respect

Go and perform a ceremony of respect! You've earned it. The artist in you deserves it. Celebrating your audition is vital because it commemorates everything you have worked on and accomplished.

The Subtees Process

In the chapter *Components of an Audition*, I discussed creating a causative routine for auditioning. One of the steps in the causative routine discusses the subtees process, which begins when you receive sides for an audition or working on a new role.

Generally speaking, theater acting is more indicative of language—the words the actor says—and ensuring that their communication lands. Film acting is more indicative of what the actor does not say, but what is conveyed through nonverbal emotions. It is driven by and rooted in an actor's subtext.

What is subtext? For me, the word "sub" means hidden beneath, the stuff that's below the surface. "Text" refers to the narrative that one creates in one's own mind. Subtext is the narrative below the surface.

The scripted dialogue is the obvious event of the scene—it's what we think is going on. The subtext reveals the real event of the scene because it is the characters' unspoken thoughts—what they really believe. These unspoken thoughts can be positive or negative.

I've created a technique called the Subtees Process to help you understand how to develop the unspoken life of the character that will serve you whether you are working in stage, film or television. This process helps build a character and scene from scratch, utilizing the subtext you discover, the character history you create, the questions you ask and your **Imagination** and instincts. Through this process, you will identify the real event of a scene and learn how to communicate this through your performance. "Subtees" is a play on the words "Subtext" and Super Sticky Post-it° Notes.

One of the keys to the creativity kingdom is your **Imagination**. I'm going to give you the definition again from Webster's Dictionary because it is important: "We would define **Imagination** to be the will working on the materials of memory, not satisfied with following the order prescribed by nature, or suggested by accident, it selects the parts of different conceptions, or objects of memory, to form a whole, more pleasing, more terrible or more awful than has ever been presented in the ordinary course of nature."

One of the most important elements of the Subtees Process is to use your **Imagination** and not self-censor. Extensive contemplation is unnecessary. ***Be On Go!*** We human beings know what we know, and we generally know more than we give ourselves credit for. Trusting yourself is hugely important. It's one of the most challenging aspects of creating anything artistic—especially acting.

Remember what Ralph Waldo Emerson said: "Abide by our spontaneous impression with good-humored inflexibility then most when the whole cry of voices is on the other side."

I like to say: "It is my belief that you are a genius until proven otherwise."

And one more way of saying this, attributed to Albert Einstein: "Everybody is a genius. But if you judge a fish by its ability to climb a tree, it will live its whole life believing that it is stupid."

Materials Needed to Create a Successful Subtees Process Experience:

- Five different colored sets of Super Sticky Post-it® Notes
- Pen or pencil
- A blank wall or an 18" x 24" artist's sketchpad
- Your *Imagination*

To illustrate the Subtees Process, we'll use a scene written by one of my students, Kelly Tighe:

INT. LOS ANGELES HOUSE - DAY

Emma, 30s, is luxuriating in a tub at her lover's place. She holds a drink in her hand. David, 30s, lies by the tub and massages her feet.

EMMA

Oh, that feels so good. I've always loved it when you did that.

DAVID

Yeah?

EMMA

Yeah.

DAVID

This little piggy went to market.

David nibbles on Emma's little toe, and she laughs loudly and uncontrollably.

EMMA

Oh, stop it, David! You're killing me! I can't take it!

David nibbles on the next toe. Emma howls with laughter.

DAVID

And this little piggy stayed home.

They both laugh out loud. Just then, David looks up.

EMMA

What?

DAVID
(panicked)

I think I heard a noise. Be quiet.

EMMA

WHAT? Did someone just open your door?

David puts his hand over Emma's mouth.

DAVID

SHHH.

EMMA
(whispers)

Who is that? I thought you said you lived alone.

DAVID

Okay, I lied, but my wife wasn't supposed to be back until Monday.

EMMA

Your wife?! What the hell, David? Go out there.

DAVID

Wait.

EMMA

Don't be a wimp. Go out there and handle this, for God's sake. I can't believe you lied to me.

DAVID

Okay, okay.

From the other side of the bathroom door, Caroline speaks.

CAROLINE

Is someone in there, David?

DAVID

Yes.

CAROLINE

I knew it. Who is it?

Emma freaks out.

DAVID

You don't know her.

CAROLINE

The hell I don't. Who the hell is in there?

EMMA

(in a British accent)

My name is Trini. I'm just visiting from London.

CAROLINE

Get your ass out here right now, you cheating whore.

EMMA

Oh dear. This is quite a mix-up. I was told that this was an Airbnb. This is my first time in the United States. There must be some sort of mistake.

CAROLINE

Yeah. You mistakenly slipped and landed on my husband's "lap."

EMMA

Oh. That's a respectful way of putting it. Well, I can not tell a lie. I did indeed have relations with your husband, but to be fair, ma'am, I did not know he was your husband. I thought he was the Airbnb owner, which doesn't make me sound all that much better...

Caroline bursts through the door, and, after a struggle, pushes past David.

CAROLINE

Emma?!

EMMA

Caroline?!

CAROLINE

You're straight?!

EMMA

You're married AND straight?! How could you not tell me?!

There are six steps to the Subtees Process:

STEP 1

When You Get Your Sides:

- Look at the show to understand its style and tone.
- Research the showrunners, producers, writers, casting directors and actors.

After printing up your sides, write out the entire scene on a set of Super Sticky Post-it® Notes and place them on the wall or the artist's sketchpad (top to bottom, left to right).

Emma, 30s, is luxuriating In a tub at her lover's place. She holds a drink in her hand.

EMMA

Oh, that feels so good. I've always loved It when you did that.

DAVID

Yeah?

EMMA

Yeah.

DAVID

This little piggy went to market.

He nibbles her little toe, and she laughs loudly and uncontrollably.

EMMA

Oh, stop It, David! You're killing me! I can't take It!

David nibbles on the next toe. Emma howls with laughter.

DAVID

And this little piggy stayed home.

They both laugh out loud. Just then, David looks up.

EMMA

What?

DAVID

I think I heard a noise. Be quiet.

EMMA

WHAT? Did someone just open your door?

David puts his hand over Emma's mouth.

DAVID
SHHH.

EMMA
Who is that? I thought you said you lived alone.

DAVID
Okay, I lied, but my wife wasn't supposed to be back until Monday.

EMMA
Your wife?! What the hell, David? Go out there.

DAVID
Wait.

EMMA
Don't be a wimp. Go out there and handle this, for God's sake. I can't believe you lied to me.

DAVID

Okay, okay.

From the other side of the bathroom door, Caroline speaks.

CAROLINE

Is someone in there, David?

DAVID

Okay, I lied, but my wife wasn't supposed to be back until Monday.

CAROLINE

Is someone in there, David?

DAVID

Yes.

CAROLINE

I knew It. Who is It?

Emma freaks out.

DAVID

You don't know her.

CAROLINE

The hell I don't. Who the hell is in there?

EMMA

(in a British accent)
My name is Trini. I'm just visiting from London.

CAROLINE

Get your ass out here right now, you cheating whore.

EMMA

Oh dear. This is quite a mix-up. I was told that this was an Airbnb. This is my first time in the United States. There must be some sort of mistake.

CAROLINE

Yeah. You mistakenly slipped and landed on my husband's "lap."

EMMA

Oh. That's a respectful way of putting it. Well, I can not tell a lie. I did indeed have relations with your husband, but to be fair, ma'am, I did not know he was your husband. I thought he was the Airbnb owner, which doesn't make me sound all that much better...

Caroline bursts through the door, and, after a struggle, pushes past David.

CAROLINE

Emma?!

EMMA

Caroline?!

CAROLINE

You're straight?!

EMMA

You're married AND straight?! How could you not tell me?!

Read the entire scene out loud. Once you get to the end of the scene, write out the history for your character on another set of Super Sticky Post-it® Notes.

What's the History of My Character?

Ask the Next Question: Determine the history of the character from what the writer has given you. All it takes is one word from the script to create a revolution. Just continue to **Ask the Next Question.**

Let's focus on Emma's history.

What's the relationship between Emma and David? Why is Emma having a relationship with David? How long have they been in a relationship together? What's the extent of Emma and Caroline's relationship?

All of these questions will come to you very quickly if you don't doubt your first impressions. These questions will activate other questions. Just continue **Asking the Next Question.**

Once you've answered your questions, you can begin formulating and writing out your character's history on another set of Super Sticky Post-it® Notes. Place them on the wall or the artist's sketchpad above where the scene starts.

I'm Emma, I'm 30 years old, I have a crazy job working In advertising. I spend way too much time working.	I have been having horrible experiences with dating and I've been getting really discouraged until recently.	I met David on an app and we've been seeing eachother for a couple months. This Is the first time he's invited me to his house.	I've been looking fo to tonight all day, I this Is the night we going to take the step in our relation

Once You've Written the History, What's the Moment Before?

There is always something going on with characters before they speak. As we've discussed, the scene never begins on the first line. What are the thoughts of your character before they open their mouth? You have a point of view. What is it?

Write down the moment before on either a light-colored or dark-colored Super Sticky Post-it® Note and place it after the history and before the first line of the scene.

I'm Emma, I'm 30 years old, I have a crazy job working in advertising. I spend way too much time working.	I have been having horrible experiences with dating and I've been getting really discouraged until recently.	I met David on an app and we've been seeing eachother for a couple months. This is the first time he's invited me to his house.	I've been looking forward to tonight all day, I think this is the night we are going to take the next step in our relationship!

EMMA

Oh, that feels so good. I've always loved it when you did that.

He's amazing. This is a perfect night.

Then, read the scene out loud again and write down any dark or light subtext that occurs to you for your character only. Here's what I mean by that:

Dark Subtext (Thoughts)

There is no scene without contradiction *(statements, ideas and concepts opposed to one another).* There is always a problem in a scene that has to be worked out. Through contradiction, you'll find the dark moments in a scene.

Write down your dark thoughts (those that evoke anger, rage, sadness, etc.) on a dark-colored Super Sticky Post-it® Note and stick it next to the dialogue in where the thought occurs. Some examples of dark subtext: "I can't believe he lied to me." "Why would you bring me to your wife's house?" "I've lost all respect for you."

Light Subtext (Thoughts)

All your reactions can't be dark, so you must find the light moments in a scene.

Write down your light thoughts (those that evoke happiness, gratitude, levity, etc.) on a different colored Super Sticky Post-it® Note and stick it next to the dialogue where the thought occurs. Some examples of light subtext: "I love how playful you always are." "You make me laugh so much." "You know how to make me love you."

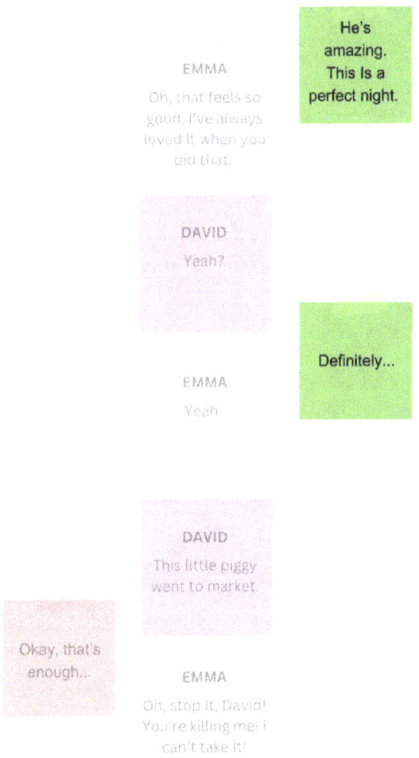

When you get to the end of the scene, return to the beginning. Read the history, the moment before, the entire scene and the light and dark subtext aloud *at least 15 times*. Don't just report your history, moment before and subtext. Give them a high evaluation. Have an experience, and work it into your muscle memory.

Each time you read the scene aloud, you will discover more about it. As a result, you'll continue expanding upon your character's history, adding more and/or replacing subtext throughout the scene—again, for your character only. Doing Step 1 at least 15 times gives you an opportunity to explore, discover and start building a solid foundation for creating your character.

Before we get into Steps 2-6, be advised: you must have a scene partner/buddy to read the other characters in the scene—you can't do it on your own. Kindly let them know that their only job is to read, not to direct you, criticize you or offer suggestions for your creative process.

STEP 2

Bring in someone to help you in person, or have them read with you over a video conferencing program. Provide them with a copy of the sides and let them read the other characters' dialogue while you read your character's history, moment before, dialogue and subtext out loud from the wall or the artist's sketchpad, still giving value and evaluation to everything you've written.

I'm Emma, I'm 30 years old, I have a crazy job working In advertising. I spend way too much time working.

I have been having horrible experiences with dating and I've been getting really discouraged until recently.

I met David on an app and we've been seeing eachother for a couple months. This Is the first time he's invited me to his house.

I've been looking forward to tonight all day, I think this Is the night we are going to take the next step in our relationship!

He's amazing. This Is a perfect night.

EMMA

Oh, that feels so good. I've always loved It when you did that.

DAVID

Yeah?

Definitely...

EMMA

Yeah.

DAVID

This little piggy went to market.

Okay, that's enough...

EMMA

Oh, stop It, David! You're killing me! I can't take It!

DAVID

Okay, I lied, but my wife wasn't supposed to be back until Monday.

You're a fucking liar!

EMMA

Your wife?! What the hell, David? Go out there.

DAVID

Wait.

You have got to be kidding me, you coward!

EMMA

Don't be a wimp. Go out there and handle this, for God's sake. I can't believe you lied to me.

DAVID

Okay, okay.

CAROLINE

Is someone in there, David?

DAVID

Okay, I lied, but my wife wasn't supposed to be back until Monday.

Wow. You're an asshole.

CAROLINE

Is someone in there, David?

DAVID

Yes.

CAROLINE

I knew It. Who is It?

DAVID

You don't know her.

Oh no, she's coming in here...

CAROLINE

The hell I don't. Who the hell is in there?

Okay, you can do this...

EMMA

(in a British accent)
My name is Trini. I'm just visiting from London.

CAROLINE

Get your ass out here right now, you cheating whore.

She's buying it, keep going!

EMMA

Oh dear. This is quite a mix-up. I was told that this was an Airbnb. This is my first time in the United States. There must be some sort of mistake.

CAROLINE

Yeah. You mistakenly slipped and landed on my husband's "lap."

She's being a lot nicer than I would be...

EMMA

Oh. That's a respectful way of putting it. Well, I can not tell a lie. I did indeed have relations with your husband, but to be fair, ma'am, I did not know he was your husband. I thought he was the Airbnb owner, which doesn't make me sound all that much better...

Do this step at least five or more times with your scene partner.

STEP 3

Turn away from the wall or put your sketchpad down and pick up a clean copy of your sides. Read with your scene partner again with the same process as before, except this time, recite the history, moment before and subtext out loud from memory. You are reading your character's dialogue from the sides in your hands. Some people discover they are off-book during this step.

The point is to discover how much of your character's history and subtext you have retained. To what extent has that information made its way into your body so that you can continue having an experience?

Do this step at least five or more times with your scene partner.

STEP 4

The scene and the subtext should be in you now. You've created a pattern of understanding and certainty about the scene. You've made it personal and specific. You've empowered yourself to abide by your spontaneous impression with good-humored inflexibility.

Now, you can act the scene without saying the history, moment before and subtext aloud. Just act the scene with your partner—at least five or more times.

Note: At the end of Step 4, if you find that there is still confusion or mystery with the scene or your performance, then go back and repeat Steps 2 and 3.

STEP 5

Reverse roles and read the other part(s) in the scene, and have your partner read your character's lines. Hearing your scene partner read your character may give you additional insight.

Act the scene five times with your scene partner.

STEP 6

Have your scene partner film you. By playing back the recording, you can assess your work to this point.

When you look at the playback, does your performance represent the product you wanted to create? In other words, is what you worked on in Steps 1-5 clearly being delivered on camera?

This is also a good time to work out the technical aspects if this is for an audition or self-tape:

- Multiple characters in the scene and how to spot them
- Whether or not to play within the frame
- Use of props (actual or implied off-screen)
- How to slate and impinge with your slate
- **Life Force**: Your presence on camera. Are you alive? Do you look comfortable? Or are you afraid/timid/fidgety?
- After going through this entire process, you are confident and prepared to deliver your product. The most important thing at this point is to let it go. At this point it should be in your bones and feel like second nature. If it doesn't, then go back and see where you lost the reality or where your confidence waned. Don't be afraid to do it again. Go for it!

Voice Work, Part I

I went to an audition recently, and a well-established casting director who has been in the business for 20 years asked, "Why aren't actors training like they used to?"

There was a time when actors were trained not only in acting but also in dance and voice. Nowadays, most actors typically don't start in theater. Their training is on video, film or television, so no one pushes them to get proper voice training. Because they don't learn to use their voice properly, their voices have no **Life Force**, no power. It's hard to hear them. This is true whether you're young or old. The point is that all actors need to have possession of their voices and the ability to not be limited by their default sound.

In my opinion, acting teachers, agents and managers should be directing students to voice classes, not necessarily to sing, but to develop that muscle. Your voice is just as important as your ability to act.

A student in the third act of her life (60+) is doing a cold song on stage. Richard stops them.

RICHARD

Let me just hear the lyrics of the song.

The student recites the lyrics.

RICHARD

Do you hear the difference between what you just said and what you sang?

STUDENT

I do.

RICHARD

Say the lyrics again.

The student recites the lyrics again.

RICHARD

I want you to breathe and stop fidgeting with your shirt. All of that physical energy you're expending is taking away from your ability to get to your emotions. Let your hands hang down and relax as much as you can. Now, just say the lyrics.

The student recites the lyrics again.

RICHARD

Go back to the beginning and sing the lyrics.

The student sings, then laughs.

RICHARD

Why are you laughing?

STUDENT

Because singing isn't something I do.

RICHARD

But singing is something you *can* do. You're not trying to sing like Ella Fitzgerald or anything like that. We're just trying to get your voice. I'm not concerned about the notes—I just want to hear you produce this sound. Okay? Once again.

The student sings.

RICHARD

Breathe. Take a breath after each line. Start over.

The student sings again.

RICHARD

Okay, good. I know this is challenging because you have never really taken the time to work on your voice. And the benefit of working on your voice is that your casting will expand if you have at least some sense of control over your voice. You could play the caring grandmother with a voice that doesn't have any power. Or, you could play the matriarch of a family if you had a voice with some power and substance. Do you understand the difference in the casting?

STUDENT

I do. You're saying that I can be a youthful grandmother who is running with the kids.

RICHARD

Yes. You could be the sweet little grandmother sitting at home with your grandbabies, and your soft voice would work for that. But for you to play the matriarch—someone who's running a business, someone who's at the top of the family—that's a voice that demands attention, control and power...a voice that can stop you in your tracks. There are a lot of those kinds of shows on TV. As a matter of fact, Vanessa Bell Calloway is on a show right now called *The Black Hamptons*. There's a possibility for the grandmother to be the head of that household. The way you get cast in that kind of role is to have a voice that makes us believe you have that power.

Voice Work, Part II

A scene just went up, and Richard is in the middle of an assessment.

RICHARD

I want you to look up the word volitional.

STAGE MANAGER

I got it.

RICHARD

What does it mean?

STAGE MANAGER

Volitional: Done of one's own will, or choosing, deliberately decided or chosen, under conscious control.

RICHARD

Conscious control. The difference between film and stage is that the stage is volitional. It is understanding that as I'm talking to this room, I'm talking to the back row because that's the stage I'm on. And if I come into this room for the first time and stand here, I test the reverb and listen. I hear ambient noise, whether from the air conditioning or the fans in the lights, and that is part of the reality I have to deal with for my

VOICE WORK PART II

communication to be effective. Study and training are important because in a close-up with microphones…

(speaks softly)

…I can talk to you like this. And we can have a whole conversation in an intimate situation. But that student back there can't hear me that well.

(speaks louder)

When I understand the stage I'm on, I can talk to you like this and still have the same intention, because I know this stage is different from the film and television stage. Does that make sense?

STUDENT 1

Yes, it does.

RICHARD

You have to learn to act on the stage you're on. Learning how to act on this stage gives you intention because you have to connect to your balls. I'm serious. I went to this opera voice coach in New York, and he was trying to get me to connect to my diaphragm. And he said, "Turn around." And he put his finger right on my anus. I had jeans on, but he put it right where my anus would be and said, "Sing." I said, "What?" He said, "Sing." I said, "How the hell am I gonna sing with your finger in my ass?!" He said, "Young man, be mature and just sing." So, I sang with a finger pressed against my ass. But what he was trying to say was he needed to feel the connection between me pulling down and using my diaphragm. It was a very uncomfortable moment, but I did get the point...no pun intended! I mean, I got the point of what he was trying to say about connecting to your diaphragm. Working in television alone, you don't get that training. You don't need the voice as much because they have mics to pick it up, and they can turn it up, amplify it and use all kinds of tricks. On television, you don't really know who has a great voice and who doesn't.

(to the student on the stage)

How long ago did I speak to you about your voice?

STUDENT 1

(softly)

Probably a while ago.

The student catches themself and speaks with more volume.

STUDENT 1

Probably a while ago.

RICHARD

Right. But that has to be a conscious thing because your deal is to be consciously:

(imitates their soft voice)

"A while ago."

(back to normal)

See? It's all in your chest, as opposed to in your womb. It has to be there. Once you understand that, you will be sexier, a leader, more powerful and more intentional. When you walk in the door, people will feel your energy. You can hear Angela Bassett in the Roman Colosseum because she's trained on the stage. Yet, she knows how to work on film, too. Do you see what I'm saying?

STUDENT 1

Yeah, I see what you're saying.

RICHARD

My point is that you have to do the work so that your voice can match everything else in power, volition and intentionality.

STUDENT 1

Yes. I was just talking about that today with my mom. So it's resonating right here with me.

RICHARD

Did you do any work at all with your voice? Did you reach out? Did you work with somebody?

STUDENT 1

No, I haven't worked with anybody.

RICHARD

You have to work with somebody because a lot of it is psychological—how we were raised and our role in our families. A daddy's girl sounds like a daddy's girl. There's a little voice she puts on, and she tries to please her daddy and stuff. That sound becomes the default sound, but it's not their voice. It's just an affectation, what they did to control their world and how they got what they needed. Then you become an actress, and unless you understand what role you were cast in your family and why, you will always default to how you were trained. You have to understand your casting before you can change it.

I want you to think about what your casting was in your family. Were you the martyr? Were you the scapegoat? Were you the hero? Were you the victim? Were you the first, second or third child? Did you have to fight for what you wanted? Did you acquiesce to get what you wanted? Were you muted? Do you see what I'm saying?

All those things affect how you sound and what you learn because if you're tall and proud because people empowered you to be that way, then you don't sit in your diaphragm. If you sit in your diaphragm, your voice becomes weak and ineffective because you have no air to speak. Voice is very, very important.

STUDENT 2

If we're not working with a vocal coach, do you think we should implement that and work on it?

RICHARD

I think everybody should look to find where their voice is. Voice is a very important part of an actor's training, as well as your ability to expand your aperture and make more money. If we look at this other student—her voice when she first got here and where her voice is now—her casting has expanded because her voice is in a different place. For instance, before her casting would be younger girls. A high school girl, a college girl, a timid girl, those kinds of parts that fit with her old voice, even though that's not who she is. I certainly wouldn't cast her back then as a boss or a leader.

Your voice is money. Your voice expands your casting. Your voice leads you to other parts and roles. A student of mine gets so much work because of their voice. Their voice alone probably makes them a hundred thousand dollars a year. You should train with someone so you understand. If you don't train with someone, there are plenty of online resources, like YouTube videos. There are endless recordings you can buy. That's how important voice is.

Call to Action:

Read a piece by your favorite poet or author and record yourself. Listen back and assess your work. Acknowledge what you like first and then make adjustments as needed.

The First Prism:
Strategy

In the Preface, one of the things I wrote about was the importance of strategy, especially as it related to the success achieved by some of the artists who studied with me and my colleagues. As a reminder, here's what I wrote:

"One of the things that I learned from teaching people who had achieved a high level of success was that they weren't always the most talented actors in those classes. But their attitudes, their passion, their work ethic, the way they leaned into the teaching, the way they let the teacher talk into their ear, the clarity of the vision they had for themselves and their strategic abilities—the way they handled what I call their **Career Bus**—put them on a path destined for success."

In my experience as a teacher, I've seen the benefits some artists reap from truly understanding and appreciating the harmony necessary between the creation of art and the business of making it a viable (and commercial) success. On the other hand, some artists are put off by the idea of dealing with the business of the business. They prefer to put that in the hands of others and hope the universe will work in their favor. Also, in the chapter "Dreams," I offered James 2:17, which says, "Faith by itself, if it does not have works, is dead."

There is a concept called left brain versus right brain dominance theory. This theory suggests that each hemisphere of the brain has distinct functions, and one hemisphere may be more dominant, influencing your personality and cognitive style. Some have learned to find the balance between both sides of their brain.

Here's a brief overview of the functions associated with each hemisphere:

Left hemisphere: It controls the right-hand side of the body and is associated with logic, analytical thinking and language processing. Hence, the business side.

Right hemisphere: It controls the left-hand side of the body and is linked with creativity, intuition and holistic thinking. Hence, the creative side.

While the left brain versus right brain theory provides a simplified way to understand brain functions, it doesn't fully capture the complexity of the brain's structure and operations.

Strategy plays a crucial role in the creation process in various ways:

- **Planning and Organizing**: Strategy involves clarity of the vision, planning, organizing, executing and controlling of resources to fulfill your postulates *(self-evident proposition)* as an artist.

- **Efficiency and Effectiveness**: Strategy favors a balance between effectiveness (becoming an accomplished artist) and efficiency (exploiting your talent effectively). This is crucial in the creation process as it ensures that resources are used optimally and desired outcomes are achieved.

- **Performance Measurement**: Strategy helps to have performance indicators (i.e., how many paying jobs you get) and allows them to be measured quantitatively (i.e., how much money you make). This is important in the creation process as it provides a way to track progress and make necessary adjustments.

- **Sustainable Growth:** Strategy enables sustainable growth by ensuring that resources are used to allow continuous development. This is important in the creation process as it ensures that your career can grow and develop over time.

Strategy is vital in the creation process as it provides a structured approach to achieving goals, ensures efficient use of resources, enables performance measurement and facilitates sustainable growth. Businesses don't plan to fail; they just fail to plan.

Strategy Groups

The ultimate form of accountability is when you are so pregnant with your dream that you are totally self-motivated and can't wait to get up and get back to it. It's hard for you to sleep because your purpose so consumes you. But even the most dedicated and driven can use a support system to keep you focused. That is where a strategy group comes into play. Having a group of like-minded, equally conscientious partners can help you stay the course.

Being that *Your Fate Is Inextricably Bound up to the Group to Which You Belong*, you must choose your group wisely. The following structure will help you set up a well-constructed and effective group.

Strategy Group Structure

Meeting Logistics:

1. Seek out like-minded, goal-oriented people to team up with. This group will include people you trust to hold you accountable and that you are comfortable holding accountable.

2. Pick a day of the week, time of day and meeting length that works for all parties. This should be a consistent weekly meeting you do not miss. Strategy meetings are non-negotiables and must be made a priority.

3. Decide a location to meet, or if meeting virtually, decide which platform you would like to use—Zoom, Google Meet, Microsoft Teams, phone calls, etc.

4. Determine a timeframe for the meeting if you are not going to be an ongoing group. A successful model has been meeting for three months and then taking a two-week break between three-month meeting cycles.

5. Create policies that all parties agree on. These can be as simple as coming to meetings on time every week, having a good attitude and committing to not missing more than two meetings in a cycle.

During Meetings:

Establish your goals at the first meeting of every cycle. The best practice is to choose no more than three goals to work on in a given cycle.

After that, every meeting should give each member an allotted amount of time to share. The larger the group, the shorter the time. In the beginning of a group or when new people join, the recommendation is to time each person's sharing.

During These Meetings, You Share:

1. Your wins for the week. What did you accomplish? What did you do well? Small wins are still important wins.

2. Your ceremony of respect for the week. As an independent worker, you do not have a boss or superior to give you praise if you do a good job. It's important to mark your wins with a ceremony of respect—it can be as small as eating your favorite piece of candy. It is helpful to make a list of small, medium and large ceremonies of respect ahead of time so you never leave it out. At the meeting, you mention what you did for your weekly ceremony of respect—no need to reenact it there.

3. Your goals for the next week. These should come from an overall strategy plan you make at the beginning of the cycle that includes action items and deadlines to help you stay on track.

4. Any help you need from the group, even if it's just to bounce ideas or talk through something.

5. Optional/additional tool: Set aside an hour after your meeting to work with your group members to begin moving your weekly goals forward.

The final meeting of the cycle also serves as a post-mortem. After you each share, take some time to discuss what worked for you during the cycle, what worked about the group for you throughout the cycle and what you would like to do differently for the next cycle—personally and as a strategy group. There may not be anything you would change—that's the goal, so if that is the case, great job!

After you complete a cycle, plan a time to get together as a group and have a ceremony of respect for its completion. This can be after your final meeting, or you can pick a physical place to go out and honor your accomplishments! The important thing is that you celebrate together.

Call to Action:

Look at your life and identify the closest thing you have to a strategy group. Sometimes, families can function as a very effective type of strategy group. However it works for you and your friends/family/colleagues, gather the group together and implement the above structure.

The Word "No"
Has to Be a Motivator

Richard addresses his class to see who has joined one of the student-operated career strategy groups, which leads to a larger conversation about the importance of the word "no."

RICHARD

A career strategy is essential because things don't move forward without it. Any journey must have a destination. Otherwise, you are on an adventure, which is basically a traveling experience with no destination in mind. You have to know where you're going, and you have to know why you want to get there in the first place. And it has to be really, really clear. I want to hear from those of you who feel like your career strategy lacks energy or direction and you need help executing your journey.

No one responds.

RICHARD

That's interesting. All of you are rapidly moving towards the end of the rainbow? Yes?

STUDENT

I feel like I'm searching around because my son and I are waiting to take the Professional Development Program class that starts next month. I felt like I was wasting time just waiting around, so I tried to take the initiative to set some things up for us. For example, we filmed some monologues, but I don't know if they look good enough. I have a ton of acting and career books I've read cover to cover, but I still feel like I'm not moving ahead, and I don't want to come off as "green."

RICHARD

I get it.

STUDENT

I agree that a career strategy is extremely important, especially when you don't know what you're doing.

RICHARD

We have several career strategy groups that students have created. Have you reached out to any of those groups to join them and receive help with your career goals?

STUDENT

I'm juggling a lot of things, but I am trying to get into a group.

RICHARD

You're trying to get into a group?

STUDENT

Yes.

RICHARD

And you're having trouble?

STUDENT

Well, so far, the strategy groups that are open, the times don't work out. And the ones that work for me, time-wise, are closed.

RICHARD

They said it was closed?

STUDENT

Well, it says so on the strategy groups list.

RICHARD

You let that stop you?

STUDENT

I did.

RICHARD

(points to another student)

This student over here was new to class, and she was trying to get into a strategy group that was closed. She showed up every week to their meetings with elaborate meals that she cooked. It made the members say, "Mmm, what is this? This sure is damn good." She weaseled her way into the group. They couldn't do anything but let her in. "No" cannot be a stop. Whatever it takes. If there's a group that you want to belong to and the door is closed—agent, manager, TV series, career—you have to toughen up and break the door down in whatever way possible. Let me repeat that: *In. Whatever. Way. Possible.* Write letters. Send flowers. Send chocolates. Beg with a certain dignity, and **Humor, Charm and Irony**. Show people that you deserve to be there.

Let me share the ultimate in-whatever-way-possible story with you. Right up front, let me say that this is not the answer for everyone. This is the answer that I needed to cut through, and I was willing to go that far to get the job. In 1976, I saw a play called *Streamers* by David Rabe at the Long Wharf Theater in New Haven, Connecticut. It was one of the most frightening experiences I've ever had in the theater. Carlyle, the main character I wanted, kills two people in the play. I auditioned for that part when it went to Broadway in New York. The fact that I didn't get it and the reaction to my audition wasn't received very well really affected me. They questioned my abilities as an actor. That was a huge *no!* A wonderful actor named Dorian Harewood got the part.

About a year later, I heard about a production coming to Los Angeles. I was determined to change the narrative that I wasn't qualified to play that part. I spent the whole month, every single day, working on that character. I did a deep dive. I dressed as I thought he would, I roamed the streets as him, I talked like him. I took scenes from the play and did them in class. I made a declaration, sitting on the edge of the stage, and swore to all my classmates that I was going to get that part.

The day finally came that I got the audition. I auditioned for Norman Twain, the producer. He stopped me after about two minutes and said he would call me to come in again to meet Billy Friedkin, the director of *The Exorcist*, when he came back into town. I heard from my manager, Ron Muchnick, that he wasn't that impressed with me. The second *no!* That was devastating! I wasn't sure that I was going to be called in again. I also heard that they were looking at every Black actor who had a name to consider them for the part. I was not going to give up…no matter what.

Finally, my opportunity came to audition for a third time. I was determined to either get the job or go to jail. Because the character stabs two people in the play, I decided that I was going to take a knife with me and give everyone in the room an experience of my concept of Carlyle. Of course, all of this was within the context of what Carlyle would do. When I was called up next to enter the room, out walked Kene Holliday who gave me a wry smile as if to say, "Good luck following that." As I've always said, telling me "no" turns me on. I got even more fired up. Norman Twain opened the door and said, "Richarddddd, good to see you!" I pulled out my switchblade, looked him in the eye, and said, "The last time I was here, you disrespected me by stopping me after two minutes. *Stop me now, motherfucker!*" Needless to say, he was scared shitless. I backed him to the center of the theater. Richard Thomas, who was already cast as Billy in the play, was sitting a few rows back. I said, "*You! Bring your ass down here.*" He hesitated. I started climbing over the seats toward him. He said, "Okay, okay," and hurried down to sit where I told him to.

Needless to say, I had their rapt attention. I stabbed my knife into the stage and proceeded to do a monologue from the play. They had 100 percent bought into the persona that I created. When I was done, I slowly pulled the knife out of the stage, closed it, sat down, and after a long beat, I said, "I want to thank you, gentlemen, for allowing me to share my version of Carlyle with you. Sorry If I scared you, but that's what Carlyle would have done. Have a great production!" I got up and walked out. After that, it didn't matter if I got the part because I *Did My Best So I Could Forget the Rest*. As I said, my strategy was to get the job or go to jail...meaning that I was determined not to flinch on my vision and plan. I was determined to blow the wall of nos down. And I did. I got the part. "Brilliantly played by Richard Lawson, who pulls out all the stops in his portrayal!" Regis Philbin, ABC-TV News. "Richard Lawson swept away the audience as the explosive Carlyle!" Gretchen Henkel, Drama-Logue.

The concept of going that far probably scares the shit out of most people. But I have always been that person to push the envelope and not flinch. One person suggested that I could be perceived as bat-shit crazy. I can understand that. However, there are many stories of artists and others who have gone that far to change the paradigm to get what they wanted. Steven Spielberg, the legendary filmmaker, has always been a man of vision and determination. There's a well-known story of him jumping the fence of a production company to get a job. He didn't take no for an answer.

Walt Disney Studios expressed concerns about Johnny Depp's portrayal of Jack Sparrow in *Pirates of the Caribbean*, fearing that his over-the-top antics would alienate audiences. They suggested toning down his eccentricities and making the character more conventional. Depp, however, at the risk of being fired, was adamant about maintaining his vision. He believed that Sparrow's unique quirks were essential to the character's appeal. The studio eventually and reluctantly gave in. As a result, the entire *Pirates of the Caribbean* franchise made over 4.5 billion dollars to date, and Depp created a timeless character that continues to delight fans.

"No" is not an option, folks. It takes a Herculean effort to have a career. And you must strategize. You must hold yourself accountable. You must hold up the group. I get it. You're new. You're floundering a bit. Right now, you want it desperately. And I'm saying to you, "Get it done." Use the tools here. Choose the groups you want to be in, go to them and plead your case. And show that you deserve to be in that group. Even if you are the newest in terms of experience, you are there to do your job and make it a better group. Do you understand?

STUDENT

Absolutely. 100 percent.

Creating a
Space Where Art Can Occur

In Arthur Miller's play *Death of a Salesman,* Willy Loman desperately tries to plant a garden. No matter how hard he tries, he just can't get anything to grow. His garden is analogous to his life—nothing he touches blooms. His life is cluttered with emotional upheaval, stress and torment. Because of his desperation, Willy puts on emotional blinders to keep chasing an elusive dream. How can his garden grow when there isn't anything nourishing to use to replenish the soil? (Spoiler alert: He can't.)

Italian physician Maria Montessori was an early childhood education pioneer. She said:

Scientific observation has established that education is not what the teacher gives; education is a natural process spontaneously carried out by the human individual, and is acquired not by listening to words but by experiences upon the environment. The task of the teacher becomes that of preparing a series of motives of cultural activity, spread over a specially prepared environment, and then refraining from obtrusive interference. Human teachers can only help the great work that is being done, as servants help the master. Doing so, they will be witnesses to the unfolding of the human soul and to the rising of a new man who will not be a victim of events, but will have the clarity of vision to direct and shape the future of human society.

Montessori's theories are very much a part of my teaching. For something to grow, there must be the proper conditions in place. To grow organic rice, you need to adhere to very strict soil guidelines. If you're growing grapes to produce wine, you need a very specific climate to produce the conditions necessary to create great wine. I think you get the point.

You must create the conditions where art can occur in your life. In some of my classes, I have asked students to bring pictures of their living room, dining room, bedroom, closets, office, kitchen and car. This may seem intrusive, but my purpose is not to be nosey. I want to see what their world looks like. In some cases, there was complete chaos. Their living spaces were cluttered with stuff to the point where you couldn't even focus. Those qualities carried over into their organization, follow through and focus.

I asked one of my students, an organizational maven, to go in and assist them in organizing their spaces. The process was really quite astonishing. It was always amazing to see people have such personal attachment to "things." Stuff they hadn't touched in years. Things they didn't even like anymore. Objects that held some sentimental value. When my student asked them questions like, "Do you use this?" or "When was the last time you touched this?" they had blank looks on their faces. Unwillingly, they would eventually let go of the "things," and begin to clear space in whatever room they were working on.

At the end of the day, the organizational maven was usually able to change their space significantly so that they could actually see what they had for the first time in years. They gained something that had been lost for some time: clarity. Without fail, they changed significantly. They were usually much happier, more productive, had a better attitude, were easier to work with, saw more of a future for themselves and were more willing to be in their own space. As a result, all the things they produced were of much higher quality.

This is not only true in the living space, but it's also true in the workspace. Again, art needs a space where it can occur. It's very difficult for art to occur when there is tension, divisiveness, third-party gossip and a poor work ethic. If you're working on a set, you want to make sure that you bring your best effort. You also want to ensure others bring their best effort, too.

According to American anthropologist Ralph Linton, "All human beings live as members of organized groups and have their fate inextricably bound up with that of the group to which they belong."

If you accept that theory, you realize that human beings are a product of the group they are in, and therefore subject to the conditions of that group. If you think about the family dynamic you grew up in, you can see that you are a product of its culture. You spend much of your life trying to work through the casting and influences of that dynamic.

What do I mean by one's casting? Let me use mine as an example. Starting at the age of six, my group was composed of my single mother and sister three years younger than me. In that group, I was cast as the hero because I was the male child and an athlete, so I was looked up to by a lot of people. I was the caretaker because I acted as a surrogate husband and father. And often, I was also the scapegoat because, as the oldest child, everything that went wrong was deemed my fault. I worked hard to understand those casting traits and how they affect me to this day, and it's truly a continual work in progress. Especially the caretaking part. To create a **Space Where Art Can Occur**, I have to understand how my caretaking can be an asset or a liability, especially as a teacher.

It's also important to recognize that despite your trappings, you are 100 percent responsible for every group you're a part of. Therefore, you're not relegated to the lower conditions that might affect the group. You can also improve the conditions of your group.

Over the years, just about everything I've ever done has been a part of a group of one kind or another. I've been a part of sports groups. I played football, basketball and baseball. Now, I'm an excellent golfer. I was a medic in Vietnam. I was part of a group that originated the drug education, training, treatment and aftercare program for the National Basketball Association. I've done over 200 films, television shows and theatrical productions. I was on a plane where a group of 51 people were involved in a plane crash. I can't think of a single thing we do in life as individuals where, at the end of the day, we don't wind up being part of a group.

One of the most important things that I've learned is that the fate of that group is determined by the sickest member. I've seen it time and again. For instance, in the drug treatment world, an alcoholic or a drug addict has a direct effect on everyone around them. The addict is addicted to the substance, but the family, friends and coworkers are, without realizing it, addicted to the addict. The condition of all of their lives is lowered to some degree. Usually, an intervention is the most effective way of confronting the situation, especially if the addict's life is out of control.

As a teacher, I have taught rooms with a hundred students or more at a time and seminars with several hundred participants.

All it takes is one person who engages in third-party chatter to affect the energy and vibe in the room. If that person is not handled, then the quality of the work or the effectiveness of the group can go down.

Creating a Space Where Art Can Occur requires carefully considering the surrounding conditions. Just as Willy Loman's garden needed nourishment and proper care to flourish, our lives and workspaces need the same attention. Montessori's teachings remind us that education and growth happen naturally when the environment is supportive.

By organizing your physical spaces and letting go of unnecessary clutter, you gain clarity and create room for inspiration. Similarly, in your workspaces, fostering a positive atmosphere, free from tension and negativity, allows art to thrive. Recognizing your casting and the influence of your past experiences helps you understand how you can contribute positively to the groups you are a part of. Taking responsibility for the conditions of your group empowers you to elevate the collective experience. Remember, the success and quality of your endeavors are deeply intertwined with the well-being and mindset of the entire group. With your group, you can cultivate an environment where art can flourish, enabling you to create meaningful and impactful work.

Call to Action:

What areas of your life do you need to create a better space for your art to occur? Home, office, car, bedroom, neighborhood, city? Pick a place to start, and dive in today.

Declaration of Independence (DOIN)

I invented a business plan document called the Declaration of Independence (DOIN).

When the 13 colonies wanted to free themselves from the oppression of British rule, they created a document called the Declaration of Independence. It was a declaration of postulates they had for themselves and the direction in which they wanted to steer the United States of America. Once I really understood what the Declaration of Independence had in it and *didn't* have in it, I decided to create a Declaration of Independence of my own to construct a clear and concise path to my destiny.

As we examine each component of the DOIN in the sections that follow, I will explain how each component operates. I will also use parts of my DOIN as an example.

1. Raison D'être
2. Postulates
3. Goals
4. Strategy Plans
5. Policies
6. Guiding Principles
7. Affirmations
8. Assets and Liabilities
9. Projects
10. Ceremonies of Respect

Raison D'être

Why are you here? What is your reason for being on this planet? Have you ever asked yourself that question? Throughout my life, I've observed people whose energy was so palpable that everybody turned when they walked into a room. "What was that? What just happened?"

Have you ever been around somebody who walks through the door and they have a **Life Force** that is so strong you can feel it? You can feel the electricity. The ions in the room reconfigure; birds chirp. Dogs run up to the person and play with them. Babies stop crying. Their energy changes the room. That's a person who is connected to something compelling and strong. That "something" is usually that person's raison d'être. In my school, I teach **"Do as I Do."** I can't inspire my students to do something unless I lead by example and walk the walk. **Do as I Do.** My reason for being is clear. It's alive and intuitional. It affects everything that I do, both personally and professionally. And I can trace the exact moment I connected to my raison d'être.

In January of 1969, after returning from a tour of duty in Vietnam as a combat medic, I discovered that if I enrolled in college, I could leave the Army three months early. Fort Huachuca, Arizona, where I was stationed then, wasn't the most exciting place in the world, being 70 miles from civilization. I took advantage of the opportunity and enrolled at Chabot College in Hayward, California.

After arriving at Chabot College in the spring of 1969, I decided that I wanted to be a lawyer. Fortuitously, I met a couple of people who were on the debate team. They suggested I join, because that would help me improve my litigation. While talking to them about it, a powerful woman, who was all of 5'2" entered the office.

WOMAN

Whose voice is that echoing down the hall?

RICHARD

Whose voice are you referring to?

WOMAN

That—that's it. *You*. What are you doing at three o'clock this afternoon?

RICHARD

Well…

WOMAN

Good. Come to Room 708.

The woman was Dr. Barbara Merdes, and, as commanded, I went to Room 708 that afternoon. They were doing a Readers Theater production of *Antigone*. In Readers Theater, students "performed" by reading scripts created from plays, films, books or short stories. I read one of the parts and got it. When we performed, I received an enthusiastic response from the audience. Dr. Merdes talked to me about joining the forensics team. I went undefeated for two years and became the state forensics champion. Dr. Merdes was an important role model for me.

Thanks to the attention I received from forensics, the drama teacher, Glenn Dubose, asked if I would be interested in doing a musical called *Golden Boy*. That sounded like fun. So, I embarked on this wild, exciting, crazy adventure ride in the world of theater. The production was very successful. As I mentioned in the Preface, we were in the middle of the last song, "I Ain't Bowin' Down," when suddenly, I had a revelation—this was what I was put on this earth to do. I connected with my raison d'être, and by doing so, I gained such clarity, drive and joy that I could pour all of my being into this pursuit. That's my truth.

I have observed countless people throughout my life, and those with a *raison d'être* are connected to a driving force in their life. I look at how they affect the world around them, how purposeful their journey in life is, and how nothing gets them down. They can only be challenged. They cannot be defeated. Like water, they go around, over, under and through to eventually find their way in.

If you understand your reason for being, it's a light that will never be extinguished. Martin Luther King Jr.'s reason for being still lives on today in many people. Che Guevara, Malcolm X, Gandhi, Buddha…their reason for being still exists. It's so strong that it is carried on by others. Everything is energy. You could sit in a chair and say nothing, and people will understand, because it's not something you have to manufacture. It's something that is.

This life—this career—is a marathon. It takes a sustained, Herculean effort. In order to stay connected to your purpose, you must maintain a physical, emotional and spiritual discipline and consciousness.

Physically, you have to make sure you keep your body in order because if you're in shape, then you're strong, flexible and look and feel good. You're present, less anxious, resilient and have more energy to follow through.

Emotionally, you've done the work to make sure that you've handled all the people on your **Career Bus** so your community of family, friends and associates have all been vetted ("to thoroughly and carefully evaluate and assess someone or something"). You're clear about what your exchange is with each of those people and remain centered and consistent in your routines. You make sure to **Never Let Your Creativity Pass Through the Lens of Someone Else's Morality**. As a result, you're better suited to hold onto your sense of ethics and integrity because your reason for being is clear. It gives you insight into what you want to do, and it allows you to operate through your first impression with good-humored inflexibility, even "when the whole cry of voices is on the other side."

Spiritually, it means you're at peace with yourself because you're connected with your higher power and in the present moment. You can have good judgment about the choices you must make and believe whatever comes to you is true. You can follow through to the nth degree.

With these elements in place, your reason for being can vibrate on the highest level.

Here are some of my reasons for being; I am not afraid to:

o   Be completely myself, fail, disgust, impress, astound, disappoint, have success, celebrate, laugh with my heart, cry from the bottom of my soul, know what I know, turn on, be spontaneous, displease, break hearts, love unconditionally, be vulnerable, fall in love with something every day, build up, tear down, make waves, crash and burn, fail again, fall down, get up again and again, soar, skip, sing, dance, talk about Mother/Father God, believe in myself, be arrogant, learn, piss off, please, encourage, fail again, motivate, empower, talk back, hit, duck, avoid, confront, misspell, win awards, lose a battle, listen, change my mind, say no, say yes, admit when I'm wrong, be right, make amends, be alone, be naked, be seen, see and perceive.

o To arouse myself, and therefore others, by divine influence, passion, enlightenment, entertainment, rehabilitation and **Life Force**.

o To lead people out into the world to conceive and pursue their dreams, develop a structured approach to their careers and lives and actualize their goals.

o **Do as I Do.**

o To sustain a career through the 55+ years as I have, this is the most sustaining component.

Postulates

Postulate:
1. A proposition that requires no proof, being self-evident or that is for a specific purpose assumed true, and that is used in the proof of other propositions; a self-evident conclusion, decision or resolution; a self-generated truth, a prediction.

A proposition is something you envision and imagine. Something true for you that doesn't need proof. It's a prediction. Everything that was ever invented was a proposition.

"Damn, if we could only make sustainable light, then we could get rid of the candle. I know we can create sustainable light; all we need is A, B, C, D. Now we gotta find these things and put them together." Well, that could have been a conversation between Thomas Edison and Lewis Latimer.

Like a proposition, a career is something you invent.

If you have a vision about something and don't require proof, then you don't need others' opinions when they say, "Well, you might want to think about…"

You must give yourself a chance to fail by following your vision. So, you reply, "Thank you very much. I'm good."

But you don't have to be critical if someone means to be helpful. If the person is truly interested in supporting you, tell them to **Ask the Next Question**. Once again, using the drunk analogy (because I love it so much), if you tell them that the writer says the character is drunk, their question could be, "How intoxicated is he?" Good question. "Why is he drinking?" Great question. "What's his poison?" Oh shit. This is getting really good because your friend is helping you follow your vision. They're not saying, "Well, I don't think he should be a drunk."

Postulate: Being self-evident or for a specific purpose assumed true. I'm making assumptions until I prove myself wrong. And that is used to prove other propositions. For example, the creation of my career gave me the impetus (or driving force) to co-create my non-profit, WACO Theater Center, a mentorship program for young people from middle school to college and a teaching tool that utilizes theater to expand their **Imagination.** All of it stems from my original truth and my reason for being: "A self-evident conclusion, decision, or resolution; a self-generated truth, a prediction." Every invention is initially a prediction—something that only exists in your mind until you can prove it to be true by the actions you take.

As I've mentioned numerous times already, Ralph Waldo Emerson said to stick to your first "impression with good-humored inflexibility then most when the whole cry of voices is on the other side." The world is telling you that you're crazy. And you're saying, "Thank you. Thank you very much." Like when you get off a stage after a performance and somebody says, "Wow! You were so great! I love you!" And you say, "Thank you." And somebody else says, "What the hell was that?! You suck!" And you say, "Thank you."

Everyone is entitled to their opinion. At least they didn't say, "Ho-hum." That's what you don't want. You want somebody to love your work or hate it. You don't want to be so mundane that your work has no interest whatsoever.

For example, here are a few of my postulates:

- My book series, **Dreams Don't Have Expiration Dates,** will inspire and motivate artists worldwide.
- My memoir will become a #1 bestseller.
- *Empowered Excellence* will serve as the ultimate self-help book to motivate kindness, love, understanding and peace in the world.
- The Richard Lawson Studios' (RLS) e-learning offerings will be hugely successful.
- The RLS website will sell online classes, proprietary products, merchandising materials and published books worldwide.
- I will create the preeminent Young Artists Program.

Goals

Goal:

1. The target of a mission.

A postulate is something that you envision. It is something you conceive in your mind with definite energy. However, it can only be realized by a set of actions in a definitive direction. That's where your goals aggregate *(to bring together; collect into one sum, mass or body).*

If you wanted to run the marathon in the Olympics, as a goal, you could figuratively see the finish line of that race. Given where you're starting from, you can see what you must do to have a chance of making the Olympic team. If your postulate is to *win* that race, then that's another story. Qualifying to run in the Olympics is a mountain of a challenge. The postulate of winning the race is the Mount Everest of challenges. A postulate is a dream brought about by accomplishing a series of goals.

Here's a list of goals you would have to accomplish just to align yourself with going in the right direction of possibly winning the marathon:

- Dedicating your life to training as an Olympic athlete.
- Studying the proper nutrition.
- Finding the right group to train with.
- Finding the right place to train based on where the Olympics will be held.
- Finding the right trainer.
- Buying the right equipment.
- Getting the proper education.
- Learning the history of marathoning.

As you accomplish each of these goals, you will gain more experience that will continue to confirm your vision of winning the marathon. Your postulate will become more and more real with each win.

Here are some of my goals related to my postulates:

- Find a publisher that can handle memoirs, educational books and self-help books.
- Plan book tours.
- Launch master classes in various cities in the U.S., Europe, Africa and Australia.

Strategy Plans

Strategy:
1. A specific and detailed course of action designed to achieve goals.

Every successful business has a plan for progress and expansion. Let's say your goal is to move to New York from LA to become a Broadway star. You need to identify the necessary steps, from saving money to deciding if you'll drive to New York, booking a place to stay when you first get there, buying winter clothes, etc. Once you have the plan, you need to execute it. Make arrangements with the bank, ensure your car is in good repair, etc. You get the picture—you're preparing to make that journey.

Here are some examples of my strategy plans:

- Create a three-event strategy leveraging the popularity of the three projects I'm currently in to bring attention to the books I'm writing and the masterclasses I'm offering.
- Do talk shows discussing all three components of the three events that are a part of the strategy.
- Book guest appearances on podcasts talking about the projects.
- Hire a PR firm to fulfill a strategic plan.

Policies

Policy:
1. A contract I make with/for myself.

A policy is a contract you make with yourself. Contracts are not breakable, bendable or pliable. They're very specific. Anybody with a job knows that there are a series of policies you must abide by: You have to show up on time, dress appropriately and address people respectfully. Policies ensure a business or a brand clearly communicates its expectations and rules for employees so they can best represent the company.

Similarly, your DOIN policies must be well-defined. These are things you do daily, weekly or monthly. For example: "I'm going to work out five times a week." It's not, "You know, I'm going to try to work out five times a week." That's not a policy. That's more of a desire or wish.

Policies are unbreakable contracts you make with yourself. Those contracts keep you on a path. "I'm gonna work out at 6:30 every morning." This is a consistent commitment that keeps you on track. Just remember, you are the business you're working for.

The following is a short excerpt from a conversation about policies with one of my students:

STUDENT

Policies are everything because policy is action, and it's acting yourself into right thinking. It's a contract with yourself that you don't break. If I'm doing my policies, it's almost like keeping my emotions and thoughts on autopilot. Those policies help me have a foundation for my life so that I can go after the things I want. When I graduated from college, I had a really hard time navigating the world because I was used to structure. I also came from a pretty structured religion. And when I left both of those things, I was sort of just floating around.

One of the things that was so helpful when I started studying with you was finding a structure in going after my dreams of being an artist. The DOIN and my daily policies help give me the structure to set myself up for success. They're based on what I need to see to get to where I want to go because these aren't everybody's policies. My policy of making the bed is helpful for *me*. It's not necessarily helpful for everyone else. I think policies also build self-confidence because you're having these mini-wins every day.

Some examples of my contract with myself:

Policies	
Eat a conscious diet.	Work out five times a week at 6:00 am.
Complete each cycle of action.	Do it now.
No is not an option.	Make an agenda for the day.

Guiding Principles

Guiding Principle:
1. A personal or specific basis of conduct or management.

Guiding principles serve as powerful stay-the-course reminders. They also help you look at how you would like to conduct yourself in order to have a sense of integrity and ethics in your life.

Here are some of my guiding principles that keep me on track as a person and an artist:

Guiding Principles	
Do unto others as you would have them do unto you..	I must lead through my ethical choices.
My integrity must be unyielding.	Always be empathetically honest.
Find the Good and Praise It.	**Make It Go Right.**

Affirmations

Here are a few of my affirmations; I think they are self-explanatory.

"The great ones have amnesia."

"You have to believe you are the best."

"Your ability to get there depends on which way you are looking."

The above are all by me, but another of my affirmations is from Theodore Roosevelt's inspirational "The Man in the Arena" speech:

It is not the critic who counts; not the man who points out how the strong man stumbles, or where the doer of deeds could have done them better. The credit belongs to the man who is actually in the arena, whose face is marred by dust and sweat and blood; who strives valiantly; who errs, who comes short again and again, because there is no effort without error and shortcoming; but who does actually strive to do the deeds; who knows great enthusiasms, the great devotions; who spends himself in a worthy cause; who at the best knows in the end the triumph of high achievement, and who at the worst, if he fails, at least fails while daring greatly, so that his place shall never be with those cold and timid souls who neither know victory nor defeat.[11]

More examples of affirmations are found on page 369.

Assets and Liabilities

As discussed in a previous chapter (page 90), if you look at assets and liabilities as 24 hours in a day, there are **12 Hours of Light and 12 Hours of Darkness**. Those 24 hours equal a complete day. You can't have one without the other. Our assets and liabilities make us whole as a person.

In life, you have to manage both with equal aplomb. If you ignore or avoid your liabilities, you are imbalanced and false. If you learn to manage both the light and the dark, you are genuine, real, present and wholehearted. You become a complete artist capable of delivering full, unpredictable and compelling performances.

Here are a few examples of my assets and liabilities:

Assets	Liabilities
Giving	Jealous
Loving	Revengeful
Passionate	Sulker
Honest	Rageful
Grateful	Controlling
Romantic	Loner

The more you are in touch with your emotions, the more colors you have to paint the characters you play.

Projects

As your artistic journey comes into focus with your raison d'être and well-defined postulates and goals, you will become clear about what specific projects you need to create to fulfill your mission. Each idea will generate its own needs.

For instance, if your postulate is to win an Academy Award, we all know there is no clear path to that accomplishment. How can you even begin to get on track with that lofty ambition? What sort of projects do you need to embark upon?

Here's a list of potential projects:

- Enroll in a good acting class.
- Take a voice class.
- Join a dance class.
- Become a filmmaker to learn how to make your own films.
- Write a feature film screenplay.
- Shoot a reel that demonstrates your strengths and secures top representation.
- Follow the people you want to emulate.
- Identify the people you want to shadow and reach out to them.

These are just a few examples of creating projects that will put you in alignment with your postulate. As new ideas emerge, your projects will continue to change.

Here are some of my possible projects:

PROJECTS	
Find a partner for my RLS Enterprises.	Revamp my online classes.
Create apps for my intellectual properties.	Find a great graphic designer.
Expand my Young Artists Program.	Set up another film festival for young artists.

Ceremonies of Respect

This is one of the most important components of the DOIN. This is a long and hard road that we travel. **Your Career is a Marathon, Not a Sprint.** It requires an iron-clad work ethic that can sustain the rigors of 10,000 nos to a few yeses along the way. It requires a strong DOIN that becomes a living document that will vibrate in your hand and heart. It requires a titanium will and heart to process, pivot and proceed. You must frequently consume the elixir of celebration. It is the thing that will sustain the joy of your journey.

Ceremonies of Respect		
Small	Medium	Large
Turkey burger from Fatburger.	Go to Vegas for the weekend.	Go to New York.
A movie with popcorn and gummy bears.	Go to a resort and play golf.	Buy a new Sony Red Camera.

Ceremonies of Respect		
A round of golf.	Take a bunch of friends to dinner.	Go to Europe.

Call to Action:

Now is a great time to start creating your DOIN. Start the process. **Ask the Next Question** to completion. Write it all down in your journal.

Career Bus

Having a career in Show Business is an incredible, challenging and rewarding journey. It's also an incredibly noble and powerful profession. As an artist, you can change the world in a word, expression, phrase or an inspired moment through a song, movement or emotion. A timely and relevant story can change the course of history, start a revolution or change the political landscape. Creating art that can change the tide of the time requires you to be entirely in touch with yourself and have agency over your choices, direction and purpose.

You are only as powerful in communicating your craft as your ability to control and possess your **Career Bus**

What is a **Career Bus?**

Imagine you are driving a bus down the highway of your life/career. It's loaded with:

- Deceased People
- Grandparents
- Parents
- Siblings
- Significant others
- Extended family
- Friends
- Your gang (people in your peer group who have great influence over you who are, not necessarily your friends; for example, it could include the neighborhood leaders or bullies)

- Your ethnicity
- Your gender
- Your religion or spirituality
- Your mortgage
- Your pets

You must be in good communication with everyone and everything on your bus. People have many misconceptions about the ins and outs of Show Business. Most people's understanding of what it takes to have a career in entertainment is influenced by false data and unrealistic expectations. You must learn to handle their appreciation for what you do and what your particular journey entails. Otherwise, you will be strapped by your loved ones who don't have a clue, which could have an unwarranted impact on your career choices.

We constantly hear about artists, entertainers and sports figures who are wrongly influenced by the ones closest to them. It takes effort to teach the people on your bus.

The following is a discussion about the **Career Bus** that I had in one of my classes:

STUDENT 1

Since coming to study here at the RLS and learning about my **Career Bus**, I'm finding out that people on it are trying to drive my bus, and that's becoming a challenge for me.

RICHARD

Tell me more.

STUDENT 1

They're taking my energy here, here and here. How do I handle it when they try to drive my bus?

RICHARD

That's a great question. Some people don't even know that they have a *Career Bus* and who it's being driven by. They don't know. First, you must learn that all of these people have an indelible effect on you. What gives them permission to do that? What does that permission feel and look like, and why do you give somebody else that kind of power over your own dream?

Most people have no idea what their dream is. When you write down your dream, create your own DOIN and read it to them, their reaction is often, "Well, wait. Where do I fit in with that?"

Let me help you understand something—your dream has nothing to do with them. Your dream will *include* them, but you need to know what your dream is without considering anything or anyone else—your kids, your mother, your father. It's your dream. Thomas Edison and Lewis Latimer weren't considering other people's dreams when they came up with sustainable light. They focused on *that*. How do you incorporate other people into your dream? You have to be *clear* about what your dream is for you. Otherwise, you will wind up in destinations that aren't true for you. You're unhappy as hell, and you live in regret. That thing that makes your heart beat has never been massaged. And then, you're looking for somebody to blame when it's actually on you. Right?

So you have to learn how to manage people. You gotta help them understand what your dream is. You gotta be okay that they don't agree with you. You gotta give them time to make an adjustment. They're not all going to make the cut. But the beauty of you following your dream is that it completes you. You are fully, unapologetically and authentically who *you* are: stronger, willful, clear, alive, purposeful. That's not something you've talked about until this point because nobody *taught* you how to do that. Until you *learn* how to do that, you won't know how to help other people understand what you've grown into, which is this new, expanded, knowledgeable, strong, willful, clear and intentional you. And hopefully, you can bring them along, and at the same time, you're learning about their dream. You're learning about what they need, and you're able to give them that. And then it becomes an exchange.

But you can't let somebody drive your bus. That's why it thrills me when people in this business have a partner and you see them dance and collaborate together. They have exchange in abundance. Back and forth. This student over there has that. Her husband supports her a *thousand* percent. A thousand percent. She can be completely present in her art as opposed to people who have to go home and hide their art behind their backs. Somebody's a leading lady, and they will have romantic love scenes and exchanges in their work. Do you go home and share that? "We had a great day, and we had a wonderful love scene today." If you can't share that, you dread the day your movie comes out. You go to the theater, and you sit there. And half the time, you're looking at your significant other with fear and watching their reaction. And he's sitting there saying, "Why didn't she tell me about this?" Now you have problems, rather than him understanding what you do. Do you follow me?

STUDENT 1

Absolutely. This is great advice.

RICHARD

You just got here. You're new, and we will help you confront those people. So when you write down who's on your bus, and you analyze the relationships—especially the people trying to drive your bus—then it's how you talk to those people. How do you get them to understand? That means you gotta be ethical, have integrity and do the work. You gotta learn to put your head down and become better and better. They'll see that you're not just here wasting your time. This is not something frivolous. This meaningful occupation is one of the greatest things you could ever do. Art changes the world quickly—faster than any other thing.

STUDENT 2

Can I speak on the concept I have for my *Career Bus*?

RICHARD

Yes.

STUDENT 2

When I think about the **Career Bus**, I think of clear water. If one drop of black ink goes into it, then it's not clear anymore. So that's how I see my **Career Bus**. I think it's really important to know who is on your bus and what specific communication needs to be had with each person. I had to do long-time work with my mother specifically because she just needed to be educated. The way I talk to her now is completely different from the way I used to. Now I'm at the age where just because they're my parents doesn't mean they know better. Sometimes, I have to be the bigger person. I have to educate them. Knowing what communication needs to be had is very important. Some people are on my bus, and I spend every minute trying to get them to understand where I come from so that they deserve to be on my bus. There are other people I communicate with so many times that they seem like they're not going to change to support me. So I'm like, "Get the hell out." Or, I drop them off at the gas station, drive around for ten miles, and come back to see if they changed their minds.

The class laughs.

So it's really important to know who is on my **Career Bus**, every single one of them, and what I need to handle for each of them. Also, what percentage of energy do I need to give to each of them? Knowing these details is key, and I just wanted to share that.

RICHARD

Absolutely. And I think that is very, very astute. That's exactly what it is. You can continue going towards the things you see for yourself and be a greater artist because there's nothing holding you back. All of this takes time. Nothing happens overnight, but it's an intentional thing we must do to manage our **Career Bus**.

Bus Management

The metaphor of a **Career Bus** filled with all the people influencing your state of mind is powerful. It underscores the interconnectedness of our personal and professional lives and the many factors that can impact our mental and emotional well-being.

In this context, effectively managing these relationships is extremely important.

Support System:

These individuals form your support system. Your support system is the engine of your bus. It propels you forward and helps you overcome obstacles. It determines the speed at which you travel. A bus weighted down with unnecessary distractions, disagreements, impatience and counter-intention will lengthen your journey and make it overly cumbersome. This weight can include your family, friends and significant others.

On the other hand, with a managed bus, their encouragement can boost your confidence, and their constructive assessment can help you grow and improve. (Most people would use the word "criticism" here, and that word is discouraged in my teaching.) Nurturing these relationships, communicating openly and showing appreciation for their support is essential. How you handle a supportive passenger and a non-supportive passenger on your bus will determine the difference.

Influence on Decisions:

Your personal factors, such as ethnicity, gender and religion, are the steering wheel of your bus. They guide your direction and influence your decisions. Awareness of these influences can help you understand your biases and make more balanced decisions. It's important to respect and value the diversity of opinions, as it can lead to more innovative and effective solutions in the workplace.

Personal Well-Being:

Your well-being is the fuel for your bus. Just as a bus can't run on fumes, you can't perform at your best without good mental and physical health. This involves managing relationships, practicing self-care and seeking help when needed. Remember, it's okay to take breaks and prioritize your health.

Financial Stability:

Financial responsibilities, like a mortgage, rent or car payments, are the maintenance costs of your bus. Regular maintenance ensures a smooth journey. Similarly, financial stability reduces stress and allows you to focus on your career. It's important to manage your finances wisely, plan for the future and seek professional advice if needed.

Work-Life Balance:

Lastly, maintaining a healthy work-life balance keeps your bus clean and comfortable. It makes the journey more enjoyable. This involves setting boundaries, making time for hobbies and relaxation and not letting work consume all your time and energy. The most important part of this is having a ceremony of respect to mark your progression and your wins.

Each element in your **Career Bus** plays a crucial role. Effectively managing them can lead to a smoother and more successful career journey. It's your bus, and you're the driver. You have the power to decide who and what influences your journey.

Remember, it's a two-way street. Just as you seek their support, they, too, might need yours at times. Mutual respect and understanding form the basis of these relationships.

Career Bus Chart

As you can tell, your **Career Bus** has a lot of aspects. The best way to manage it isn't in your head—it's best to get it down on paper or in a spreadsheet.

In life there are a plethora of possibilities of people that you have to confront, and a multitude of ways that you can confront them. The following chart on page 298 is an example of five select **Career Bus** situations that, as a teacher, I have encountered over the years. Hopefully, these examples will help you when crafting your bus management chart.

Before you check out the **Career Bus** chart, here's a breakdown of each column:

Column I: Person, Place or Thing

List the person, place or thing and rate each item from zero (0) to four (4):

- A Hater (0): This person/place/thing flat-out doesn't serve you.
- Someone on the fence (1): It's like someone sitting in the back of the bus with their arms folded. They aren't saying anything directly, but the look on their face tells you everything you need to know. They aren't happy and might be headed to "Hatersville."
- Someone who lives in the kingdom (2): This person/place/thing is in and around your universe, not

necessarily harming you, but they aren't exactly contributing either.

- A strong believer (3): Someone or something you can call on who will be there for you. You have heard them say positive things about you (person) or fill you with positive energy (place, thing).

- A protector of the kingdom (4): This is ideally where you want your entire bus to be. Not just rooting for you but looking out for you. They have your back even when you're not around—they're your ride-or-die friends.

Column II: What Happened?

What is the instance or situation that comes to mind when you think of this person, place or thing? Is it a positive or negative memory? Usually, these come easily and don't require a lot of thought.

Column III: How Did This Affect You?

Did that offhand comment at Christmas make you second-guess getting an agent? Did that encouraging note from your dad give you the boost you needed to take a chance on your dream? Some areas these bus riders affect include self-esteem, ambitions, finances and personal relationships. If you can think of more, name them.

Column IV: My Part

Now it's time to look at the part *you* played in this. Here, we look at your character assets (things about you that are advantageous and possibly need management) and character liabilities (things that definitely need management and perhaps could be disadvantageous).

For example, what is your role if your agent is not getting you out on auditions? Are you afraid to ask them questions about what they need to pitch you? Is your work ethic lacking? Are there pictures you may need to take, footage you need to create or training you need to brush up on? If you feel that your parents have too much say over your life, do you owe them money? Have you been dishonest about your life and dream with them? This part requires a deeper look—not to get down on yourself but to take responsibility. Take a look at your assets as well. Do you have great relationships with your friends? What is your part in that? Do you support them? Attend their events? Provide a listening ear?

Column V: Solution/Handle

There is no situation too difficult to be improved upon and no unhappiness too great to be lessened. There is always a solution for any challenge, especially as it relates to your own being. You've made it this far!

This is where you review your character assets again and engage in some exercises that may be helpful. Do you need to write a letter with what you want to say and mail it or read it to a trusted friend? Should you pick up an extra job to pay the money you owe? This is the column for hope and growth, where you look at the best parts of yourself and lean into improving the quality of your life and the people, places, and things on your bus.

This may also be the moment that you decide that certain individuals should no longer be on your bus. This is the last resort when resolving the situation is impossible, and further contact with them will only prove even more toxic. They've got to go...with love, of course.

Person/Place/Thing What is your relationship? 4=Protectors of the kingdom 3=Strong believers 2=People who live in the kingdom 1=On the fence 0=Haters	What Happened?	Effects: -Self-Esteem -Finances -Ambitions -Relationships -Etc.	My Part: (Character Assets or Liabilities) -Courageous -Confident -Honest -Clear Communicator -Selfishness -Dishonesty -Jealousy -Fear of: Failure, Abandonment Etc.	Solution How did you help "Make It Go Right"? -Being Understanding -Compassion -Consistency -Good Attitude -Diplomacy Etc.
Best Friend - 0	He slept with my girlfriend the day after we broke up. She told me.	**Self-Esteem** - Devastating betrayal. **Finances** - Outstanding loan to (ex-)friend. **Ambitions** - Overlooked covert sabotage and undermining. **Personal Relationships** - Drove wedges in my real friendships.	**Painting Red Flags White:** I always knew something was wrong, but I didn't trust my friends or my instincts. **Dishonest:** I made excuses for him. **Fear (Failure/Success):** Examine my attachment to him.	**Understanding:** Toxic relationship. Off the Bus! **Communication:** Respectful adult confrontation **Work Ethic:** Work toward honoring my own values **Attitude:** Process, pivot and proceed!

295

Husband - 1	I'm 27 and living my dream—which is a lot of work. He wants to focus on family and curb my ambitions.	**Self-Esteem** - I feel deceived and fearful for my marriage. **Finances** - I make more money than he does. **Ambitions** - His attitude threatens my dream, my purpose and my marriage. **Relationships** - The conflict creates or exacerbates work and family tensions.	**Selfishness** - What do I want, and what am I willing to sacrifice? **Dishonest** - I feel like I have to hide my passion. **Fear (Failure/Success)** - I'm starting to feel trapped.	**Understanding** - To share my life, I need confidence and trust on both sides. **Communication - *Communication is the Solvent for Everything.*** A therapist, outside group, or other third party might help. **Work Ethic** - Demonstrate how important this dream is for me. **Attitude** - Gratitude over expectations.
Religion - 2	My father is a pastor from a long line of preachers. Father: "Good Christian girls don't play prostitute roles and take their clothes off."	**Self-Esteem** - His comments hurt my self-esteem and undermine my confidence. **Finances** - My insecurities limit my opportunities. **Ambitions** - It makes me question my purpose, my dream and myself. **Relationships** - It makes me not want to visit my parents.	**Selfishness** - I value my independence and freedom to make decisions for myself. **Dishonest** - I hide my art, my work and my passion. **Fear (Failure/Success)** - I have to fight for my confidence and detach from his opinions.	**Understanding** - I want to communicate about my life with clarity and mutual respect. **Communication** - Separation of church (religion) and state (family). **Work Ethic** - An ethical life is essential for my success. **Attitude** - Patience and compassion, without giving in to what others want for me.

Brother - 3	Wants the best for me but feels left out.	**Self-Esteem** - It feels good to share my life with my brother. **Ambitions** - Fear of success = fear of making him feel bad.	**Give** - Teach, share, provide a positive example. **Honest** - Share my struggles along with my triumphs. **Savior Syndrome** - Honor my brother's individuality; don't patronize.	**Understanding** - Provide love, support, leadership and respect. **Communication** - I can't do this alone. **Work Ethic** - Stay focused. Set firm boundaries. **Attitude** - I make things go right. **Space** - Let my brother come on board at his own pace.
Father - 4	Provides support and guidance in my life and career.	**Self-Esteem** - His encouragement builds my confidence. **Finances** - Happily provides financial support if needed. **Ambitions** - His pride and encouragement fuel my excitement. **Relationships** - Great relationships help me build trust.	**Courage** - Take risks. Push through fear. Live my dream. **Confidence** - Support increases confidence. **Honest/Clear Communicator** - I share my difficulties as well as my wins, which helps him support me.	**Understanding** - Provide compassion and help him understand me. **Communication** - Share my DOIN with my father. Tell him my dreams and plans and how important his support is to me. **Work Ethic** - I need ethics and integrity to stay my course. **Attitude** - Maintain good spirits around friends and family. Show gratitude for their support. **Give** - Support my dad in his purpose and dreams.

Call to Action:

Time to chart your **Career Bus**! Follow the chart above and identify the persons/places/things on your bus. Be thorough and honest in your identification.

Take a look in your universe and see who you need to praise and who you have to handle.

With care-frontation and diplomacy, have the courage to address everyone on your bus appropriately.

Whose Career Do You Want to Have?

Career:
1. Noun: A person's occupation over time.
2. Verb: To race with urgency.

A student just finished presenting her project to the professional development class and wants advice on marketing and promotion to develop her voice and brand.

RICHARD

Marketing and promotion. I would identify things you saw being marketed that successfully got your attention.

STUDENT 1

That's good. I like that.

RICHARD

A good idea for actors is to find the career they are enamored by. Whose career do you respect, to the point where you say, "If I had a career, I would want to have a career like that?"

STUDENT 1

It's a mix of a few people.

RICHARD

Okay, just give me one.

STUDENT 1

Tina Fey.

RICHARD

So look at Tina Fey, where she is now, and create a DOIN on how she got there. And you will see Tina Fey's qualities and how they developed, and you will see the choices she made in terms of the things she did, right? Who else?

STUDENT 1

Chelsea Handler.

RICHARD

Okay, same thing. Look at where Chelsea is and work your way back. Research that and create her DOIN. Therefore, you have a framework to imagine the parts of that DOIN you would actually do. What parts of that journey appeal to you?

STUDENT 1

Oh, I see! Okay.

RICHARD

You do the same thing with anything you see that is successful, you like and has been marketed very well. Give me some examples of things that are marketed well.

STUDENT 1

Apple.

STUDENT 2

McDonald's.

STUDENT 3

Cup Noodles. They have really good commercials.

RICHARD

So you look at that company and the ads they put out there to really get a sense of how they market their company. It also gives you an example of how you can emulate that kind of marketing.

STUDENT 1

Yeah. That's really cool.

RICHARD

And you find things in your ballpark that are similar to you. There's nothing new in the world. You don't have to try to figure it out from scratch. Just look at the models that are in place.

STUDENT 1

Yeah, it's a mix-and-match and recycle.

RICHARD

It's recycled. Somebody that gets your attention on social media, what do they do? How do they promote their stuff? Look, one of my student's shows was inspired by *Shit My Dad Says*. Look at the way that was marketed!

STUDENT 1

Right!

STUDENT 4

It even spun off into a series on CBS.

STUDENT 1

Okay, that's where it starts. It was so foggy over there I didn't know where to begin. Thank you.

RICHARD

Yeah, but part of being in a fog is trying to figure out a way through it.

STUDENT 1

Yeah. You're right, now that I think about it.

A week later, Student 1 has done their research and timelines for Tina Fey's and Chelsea Handler's careers, which they present to their class.

RICHARD

Very good research you've done. What I gleaned from that is somebody who had a passion for something, and they continued to *Ask the Next Question*. Every time I see something like that, it confirms that people are following their dreams because A to B to C to D, it creates itself. The next question comes naturally. Sometimes, you get a little stuck, but as long as you don't stop and think on the move, you may try 20 things to find the one thing that will move you to the next step. You don't give up. You stay committed to the vision and the goal.

These two women just kept their heads down and continued to do the work. Year after year, they worked and worked. These are people following their truths, and yes, if there is something about it that inspires you to say, "Oh! I could do what they did," or "I can take the impetus of what they did and create my own thing which is different from that," then do it.

STUDENT 1

That's great advice, thank you.

RICHARD

That way, you can use it literally or be inspired figuratively to confirm your own path. It is more about being motivated by what they did and using that as a model for what you can do. As they say, "Greatness borrows, genius steals."

And I look at that and say, "These people got on a path, and they just stuck to it." Over time, all of you will be far more equipped to have a career—the 360 degrees of a career.

Call to Action:

Do a DOIN of someone you admire, imagining what you think their dream was. It will help you figure out what you can emulate.

Plan A Versus Plan B

A student screens their short film in class and finishes explaining their vision for it. They also reveal that they are committed to finally focusing all their energy on their artistic career.

RICHARD

Awesome. The one thing I get from this film is that so much can be done with sound, music and voice-over to tell a story because you really captured the world, the antagonist and the sense of danger. I got your subtext and what was going on in your inner life. I got what was at stake. All of those things were very, very present. All you had was a camera, a location, an event, an evaluation and you understood the beginning, middle and end of the story. Your film was extremely well done. Hopefully, it gives people some ideas about being creative without necessarily having a lot and just using the devices of filmmaking. Excellent work.

STUDENT 1

Thank you so much.

RICHARD

Do you have any plans for it?

STUDENT 1

I've decided that to really live in this artistic world, I have to submerge myself 100 percent. For the last 10, 15 years, I've been stacking chips, if you will, and now it's time for those chips to work for me so I can go out and do what I love to do full-time.

RICHARD

Okay. Do you want to share what that is with the class?

STUDENT 1

Yes. I just booked a feature film, and it's going to require me to be away for a month or so. And for those of you who don't know, I've been a general manager in the corporate world for many years. The salary is really good, but I really need to fulfill my passion and what I came out here to do so many years ago. I was able to get the children through school. And I've heard time and time again, "It's your time." So, without any reservations, I've decided to finally call it quits with my job and go all in with my artistic career.

The class cheers and applauds.

RICHARD

That is huge. You know, people talk about Plan A and Plan B. And most of us have heard throughout the course of our lives that we need a Plan B. And the one thing that I know more than anything else is that you can't serve two gods. Plan B might allow you to get a nice place, get a nice car and nice furniture, take nice trips and do nice things. Possibly. Maybe Plan B is just a survival kind of job. But if you are focused on Plan A, and you're doing the things you need to do to grow, expand and change, target things, create your own party, your own product and your own evidence—and you understand that it's a process that you stay with—then what's the purpose of a Plan B? With Plan A, you still need to make money. Yeah, okay, fine. Let's do what you have to do to get the kind of job or the pillars that can truly support your bridge—meaning that it doesn't take away from your artistic endeavors. That you have created this thing that will supplement what you're doing, but it will not interfere with it. Most people just get a job.

I applaud you for making this choice because when I look at you…I look at this film…and I look at what you did with nothing, that you turned it into something compelling, it's like, well, what can you do when you have something to work with? And because you're a writer, filmmaker, great actor and comedian with all this skill set, why not bet on yourself?

STUDENT 1

Exactly. Thank you.

RICHARD

There are no half-measures. You can't be sort of pregnant. You have to be 100 percent pregnant, and get into it. Love it and enjoy it. Make sure you have people around you who will support you during your pregnancy.

STUDENT 1

Absolutely.

RICHARD

Great work. ***Dreams Don't Have Expiration Dates.***

STUDENT 1

None whatsoever.

Richard addresses the class.

RICHARD

So, let's talk about this for a minute. What do you all think about that move? That commitment to Plan A that they're making?

STUDENT 2

I love it. As someone who quit their full-time job and moved back to LA without a Plan B to pursue dance professionally—and now acting—this is great because it makes me really hungry to do this. But I also see that it's a process and that you have to create. And I've realized sometimes that even though I don't have a Plan B, I don't allow myself to get into my Plan A 100 percent. Some things hold me back, like fear. I've realized that if I go this route, I have to keep creating to keep myself invested at 100 percent. I find this truly inspiring. It shows me where I need to step up my game.

RICHARD

Right. So, what are the elements that keep you in the highest frequency of the game? Community. A strategy group. Study and training. A strong, clear DOIN where you know what your purpose is, what your postulates and guiding principles are, that your policies are in place, your affirmations are strong and your projects are exciting. You are pregnant with this. You get up every day, and you look at how many hours a week you put into your Plan A. At one point in this class, we were looking at our career hours. There are 168 hours in the week. In some weeks, we had students putting in 70 to 90 hours into their Plan A. People were producing at a high rate. And when you're in it like that, that's what you put back into your career.

When you make money, you put it back into your career. For example, you buy a new computer or a new camera. You buy new editing software. You work on set, and you're less concerned about how much money you're making and more about buying your character's wardrobe. Why? Because that's a particular casting. You played a judge or a district attorney, and now you own that wardrobe you can use again when you go out for those same parts. You're putting money into seminars, and you're taking lessons. You're improving your editing skills. You're editing for other people. If you need to, you learn the skill that will allow you to control your own destiny so you can live and swim in the pool you're in. Vibrate at the same frequency as the thing you desire. That's also known as falling in love. You fall in love when you meet somebody, and the vibrations are in harmony, meaning they are on the same wavelength. My art is my frequency. I *love* what I do— all of it. I love directing. I love teaching. I love acting. I love helping and mentoring. I love being of service. So you gotta be pregnant with this shit. And you gotta give.

Call to Action:

Identify an actor's career that you would like to have and see the difference between the career that Hollywood helped provide and the career they created for themselves (for example, Issa Rae made a web series that turned into a network series). Take notes about it in your journal and take inspiration!

Create the Evidence

In business, proof of concept is essential when buying a new product. Companies want to know that they will get a return on their investment.

In Show Business, proof of concept can only take a few forms:

- The buyers meet you in person at an industry event and fall in love with you
- You do an incredible on-camera audition for them in person
- You provide the evidence on a reel so people can see your work

Creating evidence is vital. When you create evidence, people everywhere can see what you can do. You can send it digitally all over the world.

Expertly shooting your reel, producing your own short films, doing great auditions, shooting skillful self-tape auditions, writing your scripts and getting them produced and doing table reads are all ways of creating the evidence.

Your talent is very specific. You are unique and special. There is no one like you. You are a thumbprint. You have to have evidence of all the things you can do. The buyers can't rely on faith that you are as talented as you or your team say you are.

Your agent cannot go to the networks and say, "Listen, Kelly is really good. Trust me. She's great, and she's perfect for the part. Trust me."

The network's response will likely be, "Show me something." The agent should send them a link. They look at the evidence in your work. They either like you or they don't. If your evidence (your work) is good, then you will at least book the room, and they will call you back again and again.

Like any other business, you have to invest in expansion. One thing that prevents you from doing what's necessary to invest back into your business is money. You can wait until you book jobs in the industry to add footage to your reel. Or, you can be proactive and create your own. That takes money, vision and determination. It entails perseverance through a sustained effort. Ultimately, it takes creating a clear and concise DOIN, which includes in that plan an understanding that it's up to you to create your own proof of concept.

Thinking like a business owner, what do you need to be a successful artist?

- A pillar job that supports your career
- Earning enough money to sustain your life and career
- Control over your time so you can invest back into your career
- Finding the balance between your life needs and your career needs

We all need to make money to support ourselves, our families and our way of life while pursuing our dreams. Hopefully, and happily, we will find the *right* job that fits that bill. Is that job harmonious with your dreams? Does it support you in all realms? Spiritually, does it align with your dream? Psychologically, does it lift you up and inspire you to come to work because it is a

Space Where Your Art Can Occur? Mentally, does it make you feel trapped? Do you see your dream drifting away, or does it provide a supportive base where you can be confident about your life and the direction you are headed?

Finding the right job is vital as you pursue your dream. Ideally, you can find work that complements your field, as an editor, production assistant, acting teacher, dance instructor or voice coach. Perhaps you can find a job as an assistant to someone in the business or consider creating your own business that parallels Show Business in some way. This could be ideal— running a business you're in control of and where you hire people to work for you so your time is more your own. That gives you better control over your destiny.

It is also crucial that you live within your means so that you have the funds available to invest in your ability to create evidence.

In 1980, they were casting for a film called *Ragtime*, directed by Miloš Forman. I read the book, and I wanted that movie with a passion. Forman finally came to town, but he didn't want to see me for some reason. Usually, stuff like this is like water off a duck's back, but this one hurt.

When I talked to my agent, she told me that Forman went to London to scout locations. The next day, I went to play basketball with my buddies. One of my best friends, Michael Greenberg, asked me how it went. I told him.

Michael said, "Why don't you fly to London and find him?" It took me about 60 seconds to get up, hand him my basketball and tell him to hold on to it—I needed to go home to prepare for a trip. And that's exactly what I did.

Like me, Forman was with ICM. I called my agent and asked where he stayed when he was in London. She asked, "*Why?!*" and added that she hoped I wouldn't do something stupid. She told me he stayed at one of four different hotels.

That was all I needed—I booked my flight to Gatwick Airport and flew to England. Standing in line at a reservation desk in the airport, I meditated on which hotel he would be at. I clearly saw "Inn on the Park." I made a reservation, only slightly horrified to realize the dollar was taking a beating. It was $500 a night. I gave myself three nights just in case.

When I got to the front desk of the hotel, I asked with a fair amount of certainty if Mr. Forman was still there because we were supposed to meet. They said yes. This was about 5:00 pm.

I went to my room, took a shower and changed my clothes. I hustled back downstairs to see if I could bump into Forman. I walked the lobby, the bar, the restaurant, the lobby, the bar, the restaurant. I made that loop for about three hours. By then, I had been up for two days and was exhausted. I went to my room to take a nap. Perhaps an hour into my slumber, I had an impulse that Forman was in his room, so I asked the operator to ring him.

FORMAN
(in a Czechoslovakian accent)

Hello.

RICHARD

Mr. Forman, my name is Richard Lawson. I flew here from Los Angeles to meet you. I am Coalhouse Walker.

I would like to just meet you and shake your hand. I am the perfect person to play that part.

FORMAN

I'm so sorry, Mr. Lawson, but I'm on my way to dinner with friends. When you get back to the States, give your picture to Mary Goldberg. Good night!

He hung up!

That was a punch to the solar plexus. It was hard to breathe. I held the phone in my hand for maybe five minutes, trying to process what happened—it was not what I was hoping for. It took me about half an hour to feel present. Then, I went to the desk and wrote Forman a short letter thanking him for the conversation and saying I would follow his instructions.

The next day, I realized it was a huge win. I had the courage to not flinch and trust my instinct. It has proven to be one of the most important things I've ever done. It gave me the courage to follow my impulses. I'm not afraid to go and get what I want. Nothing beats a failure but a try.

Once back in LA, a couple of weeks later, I got what I wanted: the opportunity to screen test for *Ragtime*. I ended up being one of the final two choices. I didn't get the part. The wonderful Howard Rollins got it. After seeing the film, I realized I wouldn't have wanted to play the part that way. Howard was the perfect casting based on Forman's interpretation.

How does this story relate to creating the evidence? Sometimes, when the opportunity to show your wares or share your gifts isn't available, you have to create the evidence by whatever means necessary. If you want it, go get it.

Call to Action:

Issa Rae is a great example of someone who created her own evidence with *Insecure*. Likewise, Diallo Riddle and Bashir Salahuddin created and starred in the series *South Side*. Ramy Youssef created and starred in the semi-autobiographical comedy *Ramy*. Ricky Gervais served as an actor, director, writer, executive producer and creator of *The Office*. Quinta Brunson created and starred in *Abbott Elementary*. Identify what your evidence is and what you will do with it.

Your Career Is an Invention,
Part I

During this conversation, we discuss why a career is not paint-by-the-numbers. It is an invention—an original creation that takes **Imagination**, grit, will and a desire that supersedes failure.

STUDENT 1

People dream, but they don't do any footwork.

RICHARD

That's right. "Faith without works is dead."

We're taking those dreams that you have, and we're finding the specific actions necessary to make those dreams a reality. That's what it is. It's, "How do I take this idea and concept and make it so?" This is the same as being an inventor. You're inventing something.

Let me give you an example: I am a golfer, and when I travel, I like to buy caps from the courses I play on in Hawaii, Mexico, Cancun, British Columbia, wherever. One day, I realized that I was tired of the caps getting all jacked up in my suitcase. The nicely shaped crown of a hat gets bent and twisted out of shape when it's crammed in with all my belongings. I can't wear a tweaked cap. It'd be like Tiger Woods wearing a jacked-up cap.

So, it was like, how do I keep my caps from getting jacked up? I thought about it and realized, "Hmmm, what about a plastic container that you can shape like a cap, and you put your cap into it?" I drew it out on paper. And then, it was like, "Oh, okay. I can see that." It looked like a baseball protective hat, so I went and bought one, thinking I'd have to reshape it somehow. And this is stupid: I turned on my stove and started heating this plastic until I softened it. I had gloves on, and I bent it and bent it until my wife came in and said, "Richard, you got the house smelling like plastic! That's dangerous! It's toxic!"

So, I told her, "Open up the windows. I gotta finish this!" I put it together, and then I got another piece of plastic, cut it around, glued it together, and put a flap over the back. Then I took it to an engineer, and we designed it, shaped it, put it together and came up with my invention, The Cap Keeper, which I have a patent on.

STUDENT 2

That's so brilliant.

RICHARD

I'm an inventor. I invent shit all the time. My career is an invention. Your career is an invention. You mentioned earlier that you went to this producer and said, "I've got an idea. What if we did this, and what if we did that?" You're inventing that. If someone says, "That's a great idea. How about this?" and they add to it, pretty soon, if we look down the road a little way, you will have a completed film and your own office on Sepulveda and Ventura Blvds. Do you know what I'm saying? There's an action that you put into place, and you keep going down that road with your belief, fire and passion. You get other people invested in your dream because you have it laid out in a plan, and people can see it, feel it and understand it. Once you get this plan, it changes everything because everybody I know that has created a DOIN has taken it to their families, who have been sitting around "patiently" saying, "You've been doing this for a while. It's been twenty years. I told that girl to go to law school."

STUDENT 3

You got my dad down, pat!

RICHARD

I understand, but now you take this plan to your dad and say, "Dad, look. I wanna share something with you." And you give him your business plan. He says, "You know what? I see this. This is no joke. She's not out there hoping, wishing and praying." It's now real, and they invest in that because they see that this is something specific. It's tangible.

Your Career Is an Invention,
Part II

This conversation is another example of a career that originated out of one's *Imagination* and fantasy:

RICHARD

The one thing that I want you to really be clear about is that everything around you is an invention. Someone invented these things, and it was a willful act of creation on their part. It was an invention, not a coincidence. Apple is not a coincidence. Coca-Cola is not a coincidence. Sprinkles is not a coincidence. Fatburger is not a coincidence. Name it. The light bulb, the street light, the airplane and the carpeting. All of that. No coincidences. These things came about because something was needed and wanted.

In terms of your career, what is needed and wanted? Those answers you come up with have to be created, and it's a matter of putting the puzzle together. And if you understand why you're putting this specific puzzle together, then it's a fun game. Hopefully, it only becomes difficult when the fun factor is lost. The fun factor must be there because that keeps you active, alive and moving forward.

Now, it's easy to lose the fun because you get caught up in other things like rent, mortgages, car payments, insurance, food, gas, clothes, entertainment and the unexpected. Your dog Fifi died, and then you have to bury her. Or she's at the hospital with an unexpected tumor removal, and with animals, surgery is ridiculously expensive. With humans, it's even more ridiculously expensive.

All those unexpected things can stop us, and the well-known voices in our heads that play like **K-SHIT FM** can stop us. What I'm strongly suggesting to this talented young lady in front of me is that she must talk to her father. Until the day that she can actually have that conversation, she's not going to go out in the world and create her dream. She will continue to do this dog and pony show to satisfy some image that she wants to create and maintain with Daddy.

Fortunately, you meet a guy like me along the way who has seen and experienced the bigger picture. I've seen people get caught up in their filters and get lost for 20 years. Then they try to come back and make a go of it. They couldn't deal with it then. And then, 20 years later, after the marriage, three kids, colleges and oh my God, I can't believe this, divorce, they're now trying to resurrect themselves…and it's like no. She shouldn't have to wait till she's 35 before she's able to say, "Okay, Dad. We gotta talk." I'm just using that as an example. It doesn't have to be just Dad. It could be anything that represents a filter, be it church, state, neighborhood or whatever. I mean, what did it take for Samuel L. Jackson to play that part in *Django Unchained* and not worry about it? And he handled it beautifully. He handled it beautifully, but he's cut from the same cloth that I'm cut from.

When you are clear with your path, you know how to deal with these other things because you're handling them with evidence. Here's evidence of my truth. Right here, I wrote it down. Here's evidence of what I'm doing. Here, take a look at that. Sharing your DOIN with your peeps is like having an investment party. You can invite your family, friends, agents and managers—all the significant people in your universe—and you put your DOIN on the screen. And you put up the evidence of the films you've created so they see it all. And here's the agreement: No one can say anything until after, and then they can say anything they want. And you go through the entire thing and present your life. After it's over, it's like, "Okay, any questions?" And you sit and entertain any questions so that they understand what bus they're on and that they don't have the wrong ticket punched.

STUDENT

About the DOIN seminar, I discovered a thermostat that said I have "enough." I don't need any more, and it's sort of ungrateful of me to ask for more. It's okay for me to ask for stuff for my sons or husband, but it's not okay to ask for anything for myself.

RICHARD

Right, exactly.

STUDENT

I've been totally like, "shh, shh" to myself.

RICHARD

First of all, you have to know how powerful that revelation is because what you just included in your landscape is who? You. You've included yourself in the landscape of the life you've created. Whereas before, it was all for others.

STUDENT

Right. I like the idea of writing down your dream. I've seen that before, and I've done that before, but I've never applied it to my career. When I left the DOIN seminar on Sunday, I was fired up. I had evidence to show this director and a list of the projects that I had done over the last four weeks in this class. It was a way to talk to him, who's been my neighbor for eleven years, on a serious note about a serious idea.

RICHARD

Sure, absolutely. That's what makes the difference. When you have evidence, then people can take you seriously. You're not just a person living in the hope that Hollywood will come and discover you. All of a sudden, you're talking about something that has nothing to do with Hollywood directly. It's indirect because you're inventing and creating your own evidence. You're bringing Hollywood to you.

STUDENT

Yes. And then I did a handle because I said that I wanted to use my home to shoot, and I got some blowback. "Shoot it somewhere else. Shoot it over there." And I just had to say, "This is my home, and if I want to use my home to shoot something for two weeks, I have the right." And they concurred because I said it in a way that was honest, real and specific. It wasn't, "I'm asking you." It was, "This is what I want to do, and you need to get on board with that idea."

RICHARD

Yes, awesome. Other people in your universe are used to you being one way, and as you change and see more, want more and start demanding more from the universe, it's going to be weird for them. The energy is different, the demands are different, and the time is different, and you're not as available mentally, spiritually and physically. Not that you're absent but you are focusing on other things, so the rhythms are different. The routine is different. And that takes getting used to. You're evolving, and as you do, your world has to evolve with you. That's why it's important to share that because as you evolve and your family doesn't, they'll be like, "What's wrong with her?" They need to know you, and *you* need to be okay with you. There's nothing wrong with you, no matter what you've done. You pull the covers off every human being, and you'll find the same kind of stuff.

Change will occur because you are finding your best, most determined and fullest self. The space you are taking up now is growing, and pretty soon, you will feel more powerful. As you walk into rooms, people will notice the difference in you. Your attitude will change. Your being-ness will change. You will be more present. So get used to it.

Also, you will need some support. This is where community comes in. The people around you are starting to make a difference. Collaboration provides abundance. It's helping you to create and take up more space. The deeper you go, the higher you can go. That's a principle of voice. You wanna go higher? You gotta go lower. The maestro, Giuseppe Balistreri, would say, "Sit on it when you want to go up," so you would get the sensation that you're pulling down to go up.

Call to Action:

What are you inventing? Are you pregnant with it yet? Write it all down if you haven't yet. If you have, add more detail. You've got to get it all out of your head so you can share your vision and make it infectious.

Waves of Casting

Here's what I mean by "first wave of casting": If you drop a rock in a calm pool of water, it will create the first wave around where the rock impinges upon the water. From there, the water will ripple out, creating a second, third and fourth wave, each one further out from the center.

With this concept in mind, you'll want to start from the center—the place closest to you.

If you've never acted before in your life, and you enrolled in one of my classes to learn the art of acting, I would first take you through the exercises that help you get to know yourself. This is baked into the structure of several sections I teach. They allow you to start learning about who you are organically. You discover and connect to your natural impulses and instincts. We start with what you know.

For example, one of my students was a successful business-person who owned an aircraft company and wanted to be an actor. Well, if you consider what he's done for a living, he's run his own company. He has hired and fired people. He has been a leader and has led negotiations. He has weathered failure and held people accountable. He understood the aesthetics of this brand. My student naturally possessed all of these qualities.

To learn the art of acting, you build strength where strength exists. The first wave of casting is looking at something from the inside out, meaning that there's something you know that's true for you that you can play. You start by finding parts in your wheelhouse.

For example, I would start my aircraft company-owning student in roles that convey his experience and wisdom, like the role of a judge. A judge can quickly size up a person's character, make decisions and rule on what's right and wrong. He could also read for the role of a professional, like a manager, a business owner or a leader. That person is comfortable taking control, acting as a tough negotiator and holding boundaries. My student's natural inclination is to work in the areas he knows best. It's not something he needs to think about; it's something he can do in his sleep. That is his first wave of casting.

The second wave of casting is those parts that live right outside of you that require that same zip code, if you will, but also a little bit extra. It requires taking those qualities in the area of your strength and expanding on them—nothing too far afield, but something close.

For instance, my student's second wave of casting would be a businessman who has lost his sense of ethics and is panicking because he's spent all of his money. This character is unethical, and we can consider him a darker character. My student could very naturally play the businessman aspect of the character; he'd just have to extend himself in a new direction. He'd have to look at the pathology of an individual who's making decisions that aren't as morally driven as they should be out of desperation.

The third wave of casting is those parts that sit outside of your natural ability. Those parts require more *Imagination*, so perhaps you approach the character from "the outside in" versus "the inside out." The outside in means that the businessman/student uses those same leadership qualities for a cowboy character, for example, who is leading a gang of vagabonds.

In the third circle, you stretch your natural abilities. In the cowboy example, the student knows nothing about horses and knows nothing about cowboys. He's clueless about saddles, spurs or even how to walk in cowboy boots. He's got to work on the character from the outside in by doing the research and buying the gear: a cowboy hat, a pair of Western jeans and a Western shirt. That is the essence of the third wave of casting.

The process of growth through the various waves of casting is an aggregate form of study. You work on the first wave of casting first. You develop that area and expand upon it until you are confident, knowing what you can do and how far you can take it. Then, you add the second wave of casting, which stretches things just a bit. Finally, you add the third wave of casting. In this way, you grow exponentially, one step at a time up the ladder.

Call to Action:

This exercise will help you figure out how you are perceived. Take a friend who will help film you at several different malls in different parts of town. Go to high-end places, mid-range places and your basic working person's mall. Take four changes of clothes to use in each mall. Sit in a conspicuous location some distance away from your friend, and have them film you and passersby whom they'll ask what they think you do for a living and what type of person they think you are. You do not engage at all. You will get a very enlightening assessment of your casting range.

Headshots

As an actor, you can do very little without a good photograph. Producers, directors, casting directors, press agents, advertising executives, publications of all sorts and most of all, fans connect with artists through a good photograph. It's almost impossible to survive in the business without one. I should say without a *current* one. People want to know what you look like *now*. Not what you used to look like or what you want to look like, but what you actually look like. They want the picture to look like the person walking through the door. They called you in based on your photo.

It's all about casting. If you were to walk into a room with 20 people who have never seen you before and you took a poll of what they thought you did for a living, what would they say? What would their perceptions be? In some cases, people wouldn't have a clue, and their answers would be all over the map. In teaching, I've encountered many actors who were enigmas *(mysterious, hard to interpret)*. Well, that's great if you're playing poker where you don't want anyone to figure you out, but if you are an actor or an artist of any kind, there is a certain specificity of who and what you are that's important for people to connect with.

People want to be able to identify with you in some way or another. You have specific knowledge. You hang out with a specific group of people. You're from a particular neighborhood. You went to a particular school. You believe in certain things. You're conservative or liberal. You have a favorite color. You have a favorite type of food. There is no one else like you.

When you come across someone unique, you're usually interested in that person. You don't necessarily have to like that person, but that person has defined themselves, which generally calls for respect and interest. When you understand yourself, you can bring all those unique qualities to the surface to define yourself as an artist. That's what draws people to you. It's what makes you "pop."

The next logical question is, what is "pop?" First, it's an expression that people use when they look at a photograph of a person, and it jumps off the page. The image is striking, compelling and intriguing. It makes the viewer interested in knowing more about that person. The same expression is used in filmmaking. Some people pop on screen, and some do not. Some people are wonderful stage actors but do not pop on film. I believe it's directly connected to a certain self-consciousness. If a person's energy and spirit are outgoing, and they have an intention to communicate and are willing to be seen, then "popping" can occur. If there is embarrassment or shyness *(holding back)*, the ability to pop is severely hindered.

Headshot Template

Because this is a business, you must first understand your brand and what you represent to the world. Once you do, it's time to take your headshots—a critical tool in your marketing arsenal. These pictures are your ticket to the party, conveying who you are to decision-makers, including casting directors, producers, directors, networks and studios.

This is why understanding your casting is vitally important. If you understand your first wave of casting, you know it has a very specific look. You might be perfect for playing a polished corporate lawyer but completely wrong for portraying a scrappy district attorney. If the corporate lawyer is your ticket to the party, you need photographs presenting that concept to your audience.

Dennis Franz is a perfect example, because he made a career out of playing cops. He is notable for his Emmy-winning role as Detective Andy Sipowicz on *NYPD Blue.* Before that, I did a series with him called *Chicago Story,* in which he played a uniformed police officer, and he also played a detective and a lieutenant (two different roles) on *Hill Street Blues.* Playing a cop was Franz's ticket to the party. He was clear about his casting; you can bet his headshots reflected that.

Your ticket to the party may be one particular type of casting, but there are other castings/characters that you should also have photos of. You're the master of your destiny. After all the work you've done to develop yourself as an artist and a person, you should know what parts are in your wheelhouse.

A well-curated photo session is vital to get the biggest bang for your buck and have the results duplicate your vision. Here are a few tips:

Know that you are in charge of your photoshoot.

- If you've done the preproduction, just like a movie, you will be prepared for a productive shoot with the desired results.

- Find photographs that fit into your casting that you love, and research the photographer(s) who took those shots.

- Interview the photographer detailing what type of shots you want, and see if they can accommodate you.

- Watch shows with characters that fit the particular casting you are trying to create, and note how they're dressed and styled, from hair to makeup. Also, notice each character's subtext; you'll want to channel that essence in your photos.

- Hire professionals, such as a makeup artist, hair stylist and perhaps a fashion stylist, to prepare you for your photoshoot.

- Plan out your shoot so that you can go from one look to the other with ease.

  o Example:
    - 1st Setup: Beard
    - 2nd Setup: Goatee
    - 3rd Setup: Mustache
    - 4th Setup: Clean shaven

- Consider asking someone from your strategy group to run the session for you so you can focus on the emotional aspects of completing each setup.

Most photographers want to run the show. They're going to shoot in the style that defines their brand. At the end of the day, it's your headshot session. You must control your destiny by taking charge. That's why interviewing the photographer is vital, so you can both be on the same page.

Here's how I prepared the concept for a recent photo shoot. I wanted to create looks in three areas: Fitness, Editorial and Lifestyle.

Fitness: Mature, strong, confident, sexy, shows strength of character, appeals to young and old alike.

Editorial: Casual, relaxed, present, a force to be reckoned with.

Lifestyle: Classy, sexy, debonair (i.e. "The Most Interesting Man in the World").

Here's the template I used, and you can adapt it for your next shoot:

RICHARD LAWSON BRAND SHOOT

Photographer: Drea Nicole (www.dreanicole.com)

Makeup: Syretta L. Bell (www.themakeupsocialite.com)

Stylist: Sherie Simmons (www.sherriesimmons.com)

CATEGORY 1: FITNESS
LOOK 1

Essence/Subtext

Mature, Strong, Confident, Casual. The concept is to present strength of character, sexy, appeals to young and old alike. Fit older man.

Wardrobe

- T-Shirt
- Shorts

Accessories

Towel

CATEGORY 1: FITNESS

LOOK 2

Essence/Subtext

Mature, Strong, Confident, Casual. Shows strength of character and sex appeal. Appeals to young and old. Fit older man.

Wardrobe

- T-Shirt

- Shorts

Accessories

- Weights

CATEGORY 1: FITNESS

LOOK 3

Essence/Subtext

Mature, Strong, Confident, Casual. Shows strength of character and sex appeal. Appeals to young and old. Fit older man.

Wardrobe

- T-Shirt

- Shorts

Accessories

- N/A

Soundtrack

"Sexy Back" by Justin Timberlake

CATEGORY 1: FITNESS

FINISHED PRODUCT

CATEGORY 2: EDITORIAL

LOOK 1

Essence/Subtext

Casual, Relaxed, Present. Force to be reckoned with.

Wardrobe

- Casual Shirt

- Casual Pants

Accessories

N/A

CATEGORY 2: EDITORIAL

LOOK 2

Essence/Subtext

Hip, Cool, Jazzy, Artistic.

Wardrobe

- Leather Jacket
- Casual Shirt

Accessories

- Ascot
- Glasses

CATEGORY 2: EDITORIAL

LOOK 3

Essence/Subtext

Classy, Cool, Sexy.

Wardrobe

- Black Jacket

- Black Turtleneck

- Black Pants

Accessories

N/A

Soundtrack

"Smooth Operator" by Sade

CATEGORY 2: EDITORIAL

FINISHED PRODUCT

CATEGORY 3: LIFESTYLE

LOOK 1

Essence/Subtext

"The Most Interesting Man in the World," Classy, Sexy, Debonair.

Wardrobe

- Tuxedo

- Tuxedo Shirt

Accessories

- Tux Shoes

- Bow Tie

CATEGORY 3: LIFESTYLE

LOOK 2

Essence/Subtext

Gambler. "The man." Not to be messed with. Ladies man.

Wardrobe

- Black tuxedo (open)
- Button down tux shirt

Accessories

- Bow tie (undone)
- Tux shoes
- Cocktail

CATEGORY 3: LIFESTYLE

LOOK 3

Essence/Subtext

Relaxed, Cool, Devilish, Handful, Boss/Owner, Kingpin.

Wardrobe

- Pinstriped suit

- White button down

Accessories

- Tie

- Broach

Soundtrack

"Empire State of Mind" by Jay-Z feat. Alicia Keys

CATEGORY 3: LIFESTYLE

FINISHED PRODUCT

Call to Action:

Before you book your photoshoot, do the legwork! Use the Headshot Template as a guideline to make one for yourself.

Photo Shoots:
Take Someone with You That Turns You On

When I say "take someone with you that turns you on," I mean it literally. When you're around someone you're attracted to, have a passion for and who ignites your fire within, the energy exuded between the two of you can be palpable, and the camera will capture that. That spark of electricity puts a light in your eyes and a bounce in your step.

One of the great loves of my life was a photographer. We had a photo session that was out of this world. Every time I looked at her, I was smitten. There was a never-ending flow of energy between us, and it wasn't all about sex. It was just the sheer fun of being together and how we made each other laugh, be silly and then try to get serious. We played with different looks and different scenarios. Those photographs were so stunning and alive; they were some of the best pictures I've ever taken in my life. I wasn't just posing for the camera. Every shot had its own intention. There was a story with each one. We were impinging each other throughout the entire photo session. There was a real exchange between her, me and the camera. The final analysis was that those pictures really "popped."

Call to Action:

Look across the landscape of your life and write down the list of people with that kind of energy who could serve in that role and fulfill that slot.

Video Library

A video library consists of one-minute reels representing your first wave of casting. Whatever it is that you are, you'll have a one-minute reel playing each of those characters, so when those auditions come up for those roles, you can reach into your video library and send out a specific media clip that represents that casting. The clips in your video library are immediate and accessible. It's not something you have to create in a rush. Just like companies stock a suite of products, you have your lineup of products, sort of like Canon has a line of cameras. What's your lineup of products?

Call to Action:

Gather all the films, TV shows, interviews, shorts and home movies you have of yourself that represent your first wave of casting, and put them on one drive. It's essential to have a library of all your stuff.

Agents Versus Managers

Now that you have arrived at a point in your artistic journey where you have mastered your first waves of casting, have headshots that communicate those castings and have created a video library of scenes, the next step is to secure representation. You are not coming in empty-handed; you're armed with evidence that you can use to sell yourself to an agent or manager. Agents and managers can then use that evidence to sell you to Hollywood.

Developing a solid relationship with your team is essential for a successful journey in Show Business. That team begins with your agent(s) and manager(s). They have different roles in your career development:

Theatrical Agent (Talent Agent)

- **Procuring Work:** An agent's primary role is to secure auditions and job opportunities for their clients. They have extensive industry contacts and actively pitch their clients for suitable roles in theater, film and television.

- **Negotiating Contracts:** Agents handle contract negotiations on behalf of their clients, ensuring they receive fair compensation, benefits and working conditions.

- **Career Guidance:** While agents provide general career advice, their primary focus is on securing work and maximizing their clients' earning potential.

Manager

- **Long-Term Career Development:** Managers take a more holistic approach, focusing on the long-term development of their clients' careers. They help shape their clients' image, create strategies for career advancement and provide ongoing support and guidance.
- **Day-to-day Management:** Managers handle the day-to-day aspects of their clients' careers, such as scheduling, publicity and communicating with industry professionals.
- **Personal Support:** Managers often play a more personal role, providing emotional support and helping clients navigate the challenges of the entertainment industry.

Key Differences

Focus:

- Agents focus on getting their clients work.
- Managers focus on developing their clients' overall careers.

Scope:

- Agents primarily deal with contracts and negotiations.
- Managers have a broader role, encompassing career strategy, day-to-day management and personal support.

Relationship:

- Agents are often seen as more transactional.

- Managers tend to have a closer, more personal relationship with their clients.

Legalities:

- Unions regulate agents, and agents must be licensed in certain states.
- Agents receive a 10 percent commission. (Usually from clients, however, the law doesn't dictate who pays that fee).
- Managers are not subject to the same regulations. Managers can ask their clients for anywhere from 10 percent to 30 percent commission from their clients. For example, Colonel Tom Parker's percentage of Elvis Presley's earnings varied depending on the source of income: 25 percent of Elvis' record and movie deals, 50 percent of merchandising deals, and 50 percent of touring revenue after expenses. (This was a bad deal; never take those terms!)

As you can see, both theatrical agents and managers play crucial roles in actors' careers. And the truth is, in most cases, there isn't a clear delineation between these two important figures. Their roles often overlap, and they both do similar jobs.

Establishing the parameters of your working relationship with each is crucial to getting the most out of your team. The goal is to get to know their strengths and liabilities, and for them to gain an initial understanding of yours.

I've formulated a series of questions that I believe are important to ask in your initial conversation. Your relationship with your agent or manager can become as intimate on certain levels as a romantic partner. The getting-to-know-you phase is just as crucial, so here is a series of questions you can ask each potential member of your team.

Questions for a Prospective Manager

"What discipline do you come from?"

Why is that important? Because if a manager were a former agent, that would tell you about what they did on a day-to-day basis for actors. Right up front, you'll know they are a negotiator at heart. If they were an agent in a small company, they would have had to cover a greater field. If they were an agent with CAA, WME or another top-tier agency, they probably covered one area—one studio, one network or one company. This information can tell you something about their relationships and where their network is strongest.

If they were a lawyer before, it tells you about their ability as a negotiator. They should be competent with contracts and able to safeguard your interests. It doesn't necessarily tell you much about their bedside manner, experience with developing talent or knowledge of material, including plays or films. It doesn't necessarily say much about their relationship with directors or producers, unless they were an entertainment attorney who might have that insight and those connections.

If they were a press agent, they would have specific knowledge of marketing and promotion. If they knew many people in the business, they may know quite a bit about artist development. Their discipline (and history) can tell you a lot about what to expect.

"What are your areas of strength?"

If I asked you, "As an actor, what do you think your areas of strength and weakness are?" you could tell me. For the same reasons, this is an excellent question to pose to a manager.

"What would you say are the responsibilities of a manager?"

They should be able to tell you succinctly what their responsibilities are as a manager and how they differ from those of agents. You could also share what you think a manager's job is in your perfect world.

"How are you different from an agent?"

That's a huge one because the *average* manager is just a modified agent. They do the same thing. They look through the breakdowns, circle certain things their clients might be right for and then either submit themselves or call the agent and say, "Hey, I found this in the breakdowns." And the agent will usually say, "Uh, yeah. I'm already on top of that." And the manager replies with, "Oh. Okay."

You don't want that! Make sure your manager-to-be brings more to the table. Otherwise, you're paying 20 percent (ten percent each) for something one person can do.

"What is my job as the client?"

They should be able to tell you what they expect from you (the talent) and what they need from you to do their job the best that they can.

"How many people are on your roster?"

After they answer that, the next question is:

"How do you divide your time to cover that many people effectively? And do you feel that each client gets sufficient coverage?"

If they manage forty people, how much coverage is there? Because then, you're looking at how much money you're costing them or how much money you need to bring to them. This way, you understand how to use your air time most effectively so you don't waste their time or yours.

"What's your concept of management?"

What is the philosophy of your management company? Does the company have a mission statement? How many managers work within the company? How strong are their relationships in the business?

Think about this question like you're in a restaurant. What's the concept? The ambiance, the food, the atmosphere, the style of serving and care, the maître d's job? Is there a relationship with the cook? Does the cook come out and greet the people in his white coat like Wolfgang Puck? He actually goes out on the floor. "How's it going? You're happy with the food?" His towel is across his shoulders. His white coat has a stain or two, so it's not like he's clean. Rather, he's been in it. He gets in the kitchen. He goes from restaurant to restaurant, gets in the kitchen, and cooks. That's a concept.

"What's the development period of a client?"

This answer is crucial. You can actually say, "If I sign with you, please take me through what you think is the developmental period before it starts to flatline and plateau. How can we keep it on an upward trend?"

"How much time do you invest in an artist's career before you drop them?"

Ask your potential manager about their criteria—it's well worth knowing upfront.

"What do you feel your time is worth per hour?"

Why is that important? It's to give you a reality check of how much money the manager must make if they spend five minutes a day on you. That's a hard question to ask, but it's hard *not* to ask because if their time is worth $300 an hour, and they spend five minutes a day on your behalf, that's $25 a day on you. Multiply that by five weekly business days. That's $125. Multiply $125 by fifty-two weeks, and you get $6,500 —that's what your manager will invest in you annually (at least at the beginning of your working relationship). At the end of the first year, they'll look at what you brought in. Well, maybe they think you're close, so they do another year, and that's $13,000. Again, they'll review your performance. After a while, the investment may not be worth it for them—or you.

"How often should we communicate?"

Get clear about creating consistent and efficient communication so you don't waste time, money and resources—yours or your manager's. Hearing about the kind of regular cycle that your manager has with other clients will clue you into how they operate. And you can share your desire, too. You might say, "I'd like to check in every Friday to see what's going on." And you can emphasize that it will be a quick five-minute check-in. Keep in mind you're not just chatting for the sake of saying hi—you're giving them evidence and a new piece to the puzzle, which provides them with more options to play the game.

"You don't have to name names, but what is the relationship like between you and your favorite clients?"

Hopefully, they say, "Well, we do this, and we do that, and it's successful in this way, and these are the actions we take." And you say, "Well, that's the kind of relationship I want to duplicate because I want you to work for me and be happy to work for me. And I want to be the kind of client that comes in, and you're glad to see me and talk to me because we have a substantive relationship that produces results." Wouldn't that be an empowering exchange?

Questions for a Prospective Agent

As you can see, the questions are similar. But now that you know the difference between an agent and a manager, you can tell if your prospective agent does, too, by how they answer the following questions.

- **"Does your agency have a mission statement?"**

- "What's the concept of your company?"
- "What would you say are the responsibilities of an agent?"
- "How are you different from a manager?"
- "How many people do you represent in my casting zone that go up for the same parts?"
- "How do you fight for both of us?"
- "How many people are on your roster?"
- "What is my job as the client?"
- "What's the development period of a client?"
- "What do you feel your time is worth per hour?"
- "How often should we communicate?"
- "You don't have to name the names, but what is the relationship like between you and your favorite clients?"

Most actors would hesitate to ask those questions, because they're hard questions. But they're valid, important questions to ask.

Call to Action:

Now that you have the keys to the kingdom, roll up your sleeves and get to work, imagining the career you will have and doing it the way you want to do it. If you want it, go get it. There's nothing to stop you but you. *Let's go.*

How Does Hollywood Find You?

A major part of strategizing your career is putting yourself in a position where people can find you so you can share the evidence of your talent. Below, I've shared several platforms and described how each can serve you, depending on what you're trying to accomplish.

Personal Website

A personal website allows you to control your narrative, build your brand, showcase your achievements, establish your authority, generate interest from interested creators and collaborators and gain media exposure. It's a powerful tool for personal branding and professional growth.

1. **Credibility**: A professional-looking website instantly boosts your credibility and legitimacy in the eyes of potential partners (casting directors, agents, managers, brands, companies that see you as a possible influencer, etc.) and your audience.

2. **Opportunities:** A website allows you to offer more in-depth content, such as blog posts, longer articles, downloadable resources and even an online store for merchandise.

3. **Build your audience**: Optimizing your website for search engines (SEO) helps people find you organically when searching for relevant topics and mutual interests.

4. **Gallery:** Use your website as a gallery of your work (like an artist's portfolio). The link to your website should be embedded in other media platforms that you use.

Social Media Platforms

Instagram

Instagram can be a powerful tool for personal branding, marketing, audience engagement and business growth. It's particularly beneficial for any actor looking to reach a wider audience or establish an online presence.

1. **Connect with like-minded users:** Find your people and build your audience with others who share similar interests—and support your work and career.

2. **Market your content:** Use Instagram to promote your projects and appearances and build excitement for upcoming releases.

3. **Monetize your account:** As you increase followers based on organic interest, Instagram provides opportunities to monetize your account through sponsored posts, affiliate marketing and more.

4. **Excellent storytelling tool:** Because it's a visual platform, you can use it like a mini-showcase to promote your works in an engaging narrative.

5. **Build your personal brand:** By choosing your images and videos wisely, you can convey your essence, build your brand identity and increase your visibility.

6. **Engage with your audience:** Instagram's features, such as comments, likes and direct messages make it easy to engage with your audience. To make the connection super personal at scale, use the broadcast function to share the inside scoop on what you're up to and behind-the-scenes moments using text, photos, videos, voice notes and polls.

7. **Reputation management:** Having an Instagram account, especially a verified one, signals that you are reputable, real and transparent.

Facebook

Facebook can be a very helpful tool for personal branding, marketing, audience engagement and business growth. It's particularly beneficial for anyone looking to establish an online presence or reach a wider audience.

1. **Stay connected:** Connect with your fans, friends and family in a personal way.

2. **Broad dissemination of information:** You can publish a post on Facebook and instantly send it to dozens, hundreds or even thousands of your fans.

3. **Diverse range of posts**: Facebook allows you to share posts, photos and links to other interesting content and keep people updated on your projects.

4. **Separate business and personal profiles**: Facebook keeps your fan page and personal profile separate.

5. **Cost-effective exposure**: A fan page is an affordable way to convey your personal brand.

6. **Reach your target audience**: Facebook makes buying targeted ads for projects you want to amplify and promote easy and affordable.

7. **Community building**: You can turn your fan base into a community by using Facebook Groups.

X (formerly Twitter)

X is useful because there is an immediacy to it. Quick and to the point, for a public that responds to short sound bites.

1. **Brand building**: X allows you to establish and deepen your personal brand.

2. **Networking**: Use X to connect with industry professionals like casting directors, headshot photographers, filmmakers, publicists and agents. Comment on their posts, DM them and make your presence known by adding value to the conversations they initiate.

3. **Promotion:** Like other social networks, you can promote your work by sharing videos of your performances, headshots and other content related to your work. Unlike other channels, X has the value of being more immediate, so it's a great way to promote timely information.

4. **Engagement:** X provides a platform for actors to engage with their fans and the public. They can share updates, behind-the-scenes content and personal insights, creating a more intimate connection with their audience.

5. **Community contribution:** By supporting, helping, collaborating and championing others in the industry, you can contribute to the community and build a positive online presence.

TikTok

TikTok is an excellent way to showcase your talents—both what you want to be known for and what you do for fun (which is also entertaining). *Remember, authenticity is key to effectively using TikTok (or any social media platform).* It's about building genuine connections and providing value, not just self-promotion.

1. **Creative outlet:** TikTok can be used as a creative outlet or even a mini portfolio. You can share short videos of your performances, original songs, stand-up material or recent monologues.

2. **Community building**: TikTok has transformed into a place for artists like you to build a community and share tips, experiences, stories and ideas.

3. **Career opportunities**: TikTok can open a variety of doors for your career, such as getting signed to an agency or booking work for prominent networks or clients.

4. **Brand deals**: Like Instagram, maintaining an active presence on TikTok can help you land traditional brand deals and a sizable income.

5. **Content ideas**: You can record a day in the life, break down auditioning dos and don'ts, offer demo reel tips, reveal where to find casting calls, teach an accent or dialect, build your dream cast or share acting advice you wish you could give your younger self.

YouTube

YouTube is a terrific creative platform for you to express yourself through short-form and long-form videos. These videos can become your unique stamp and voice that builds your viewing audience.

1. **Resume building**: YouTube can serve as a living record of your best clips. Be sure to post your best performances, such as a demo reel, monologue or scenes that display your talent.

2. Discovery: YouTube can help you get discovered, not just on your own channel but also when you appear on others' channels.

3. Community building: YouTube allows you to share your skills and experiences, making you accessible to a wider audience. Be sure to respond to comments!

4. Creative outlet: YouTube can be a great place to showcase your creativity and sharpen your skills. You can upload whatever content you want, using your channel to experiment, test new ideas, live broadcast and have fun.

5. Monetization: You can monetize your content through YouTube's Partner Program. To qualify, you must have a minimum of 1,000 subscribers and 4,000 watch hours over the last 12 months. You can also earn money through brand partnerships, affiliate links and more.

Remember, social media is just that—*social!* While the platforms vary, they all offer opportunities to network with industry pros, connect with fans, showcase your work, announce big things (PR) and establish and reinforce your personal brand. Trying to be everywhere is daunting, so I advise picking a couple and staying active with them. Also, technology changes consistently, and what is hot today may not be hot tomorrow. Make sure that you're showing up in the places that are most current.

Professional Platforms

IMDbPro

IMDbPro is an online, comprehensive database containing a wealth of information regarding the entertainment industry. From contact information for various industry professionals and companies to information about upcoming releases, an IMDbPro account is valuable in gaining access to and building relationships with the people and things you are interested in. You can create a profile page that contains headshots, credits, demo clip reels, etc. However, while IMDbPro can be a powerful tool, you should be careful not to reveal too much personal information on your profile.

1. **Networking**: IMDbPro can be an excellent networking tool for connecting with industry professionals. It allows you to view the contact details of industry professionals and companies.

2. **Resume building**: Your IMDbPro account is your calling card—it serves as a resume that anyone can view. This is a crucial place to showcase your work, skills and experience.

3. **Research**: You can use IMDbPro to research film and TV projects to prepare for auditions and roles. You can also use it to research your first wave of casting, helping deepen your knowledge and providing real-world inspiration.

4. **Popularity indicator**: The on-site rating system, STARmeter, can indicate to casting directors, producers and directors how popular you are based on page views of your profile. It's similar to how many followers a person has.

5. **Organizational tool**: You can use IMDbPro as an organizational tool for your everyday business. You can find contact information that helps you fill in details and facts you're trying to uncover about people in front of and behind the camera. It's also a tool to keep people updated on your headshots and production shots from the past.

Actors Access

Actors Access is the industry go-to for casting projects. Actors and talent representatives use this site to submit directly to film and TV casting breakdowns. With an account, you can build your profile with headshots, a resume and demo reels. Your profile is the first thing casting directors see when they receive a submission for a role.

1. **Headshots**: Choose your headshots wisely. The first two photos you can upload to your profile are free. When submitting for projects, your image appears in a square thumbnail for the casting director to review.

2. **Resume**: Keep your resume up-to-date. Update your profile periodically with new credits as they happen.

3. **SlateShot**: A SlateShot is a seven-second video clip that brings your headshot to life, so be sure to include one when submitting. If you add a SlateShot to your profile, your name gets shuffled to the top of the pile.

4. **Video clips**: Upload video clips to create a reel. For a one-time payment (at the time of this printing, $22 per minute), upload performance videos to add to your profile.

5. **Optimize your videos**: The goal is to catch the eye of the casting director while demonstrating your skills in under a minute.

6. **Networking**: Agents use Actors Access to submit their clients. Submitting yourself actively can give you more knowledge about casting directors.

Backstage

Backstage is one of the oldest and most respected resources for news and information about the entertainment industry. From casting opportunities to articles and interviews, it's an excellent tool for you to utilize in your career development.

1. **Prepare your materials**: You'll need a headshot, acting resume and demo reel. Casting directors often require you to submit these materials before they will consider you for roles.

2. **Set up a profile**: One of the best tools on Backstage is the ability to set up a profile, which is searchable by

casting directors or anyone looking for talent. You can upload a headshot, reel, list of your skills, credits and more.

3. **Apply for roles**: Browse Backstage's casting notices (which are updated daily) and submit yourself for roles you can see yourself playing. Be determined and apply as much as you can.

Affirmations and Inspiring Quotes

Affirmations and words of inspiration from wise individuals can help you manifest your dreams and goals by:

1. Motivating you to act and inspiring you to never give up.

2. Reminding you of your dreams and giving you that zeal to achieve them at any cost.

3. Influencing your subconscious mind so that you can access newer beliefs.

4. Allowing you to concentrate on yourself, your growth process and your goals as a whole.

5. Creating a positive energy that radiates outwards and attracts opportunities and resources that support your goals.

6. Aligning your thoughts and beliefs with your goals and dreams.

7. Helping you stay focused on overcoming obstacles.

8. Retraining your brain to focus on success and abundance, motivating you to take the actions required.

Here are a few of my favorite quotes from inspirational people:

"Never be afraid of an author. An actor is a free artist. You want to create an image that is different from the author's. When the two images—the author's and the actor's—fuse into one, then a true artistic work is created."

—attributed to Konstantin Stanislavski

"To believe your own thought, to believe that what is true for you in your private heart is true for all men—that is genius. Speak your latent conviction, and it shall be the universal sense; for the inmost in due time becomes the outmost, and our first thought is rendered back to us by the trumpets of the Last Judgment. Familiar as the voice of the mind is to each, the highest merit we ascribe to Moses, Plato, and Milton is that they set at naught books and traditions, and spoke not what men, but what they thought.

A man should learn to detect and watch that gleam of light which flashes across his mind from within, more than the lustre of the firmament of bards and sages. Yet he dismisses without notice his thought, because it is his. In every work of genius we recognize our own rejected thoughts; they come back to us with a certain alienated majesty.

Great works of art have no more affecting lesson for us than this. They teach us to abide by our spontaneous impression with good-humored inflexibility than most when the whole cry of voices is on the other side. Else tomorrow a stranger will say with masterly good sense precisely what we have thought and felt all the time, and we shall be forced to take with shame our own opinion from another."

—Ralph Waldo Emerson

Here are some affirmations and quotes from anonymous sources to help you on your journey as an actor and in life:

"That which defines you professionally doesn't define you personally."

"When preparation meets opportunity, dreams really can come true."

"Don't expect people to treat you better than you treat yourself."

"You can't think yourself into right actions. You have to act yourself into right thinking."

"You don't have to know everything before you start something. Just get started."

"How can you be it and never see it?"

And finally, here are some of my most quotable lines—please use them to motivate you!

"Life is astonishing, incredible, magnificent, sublime, gorgeous, generous, romantic, outrageous, sensual, sexual, lascivious, lustful, charming, humourous, orgasmic, inspiring and ironic to say the least. It is also nasty, painful, dangerous, lewd, freakish, perverse, grotesque, unfaithful, horrible, odious, queer, intimidating, mercenary, promiscuous, mischievous, lecherous, predatory, perverted and obscene. Life is a sumptuous banquet, but most people are starving to death."

"Find your lane."

"Smell and taste the blood."

"Know your assets and liabilities. Honor them equally."

"The great ones have amnesia."

"The three ingredients to success in this order: politics, personality and craft."

"Middle-class values are the death of art."

"You have to believe you are the best."

"Own your secrets and claim them."

"The first question is: 'What is it about?'"

"Sometimes it takes a breakdown to have a breakthrough."

"Sickness is not an excuse."

"A causative routine is necessary to negate a negative one."

"Birth the story first. Then you can fix it."

"Your ability to get there depends on which way you are looking."

"Do it now."

"Don't give in to gravity."

"If you don't love it, how can you do it well?"

Call to Action:

Start a section in your journal to collect your favorite affirmations and words of wisdom. They don't all have to be from people in the acting industry; some of my favorite empowering quotes come from a diverse list of people, including Martha Graham, Solomon Ibn Gabirol, Ben Hogan, Edward Wallis Hoch, Henry Miller, James Baldwin, Maya Angelou, Langston Hughes, Toni Morrison, Nikki Giovanni, Paulo Coelho and Reverend Ike, to name a few. Make it a point to review these affirmations daily—you might even want to write them down or print them out and hang them in a place you look every morning.

Conclusion

Aggregate:
1. Formed by the conjunction or collection of particulars into a whole mass or sum; total; combined.
2. To bring together; collect into one sum, mass, or body.

I come back to "aggregate" because the basis of my teaching is a process that, as the definition suggests, builds on itself. Everything in life is constructed through a process of learning with emphasis on the word *process*. Knowledge is received one step at a time.

Why is this important? Becoming an accomplished artist takes purpose, training, sustained effort, passion, resilience, policies, principles, goals and a clear and unbreakable vision. Remember that **Your Career is a Marathon, Not a Sprint.** This teaching is meant to support you in having a long, successful and fulfilling career and realizing your dreams.

Acknowledgments

I can unequivocally say that I am an artist down to the marrow of my bones. The right brain, the artist side of me, is filled with *Imagination* and wonder, creativity and curiosity, passion and determination. I am that person who will start with a two-person poetry reading and end up with a 50-person musical (*From The Heart Of Love*). It was a wonderful process and an incredible production. But you can imagine the strategy involved. The logistics. The level of organization, trust and loyalty it took to keep expanding and constantly moving the goalpost. So, the left brain, my logical, analytical side, is challenged to find the balance to pull off the *Imagination* created by the right brain.

That's where my team comes in. I've managed to build an incredible team around me. I was fortunate enough to be mentored by Milton Katselas, who mastered the art of creating structure to support his creative process.

When it comes to building, running, maintaining and expanding Richard Lawson Studios, our seminars, our master classes and writing this book, I could not have done it alone. Jorge Ortiz and Kelly Tighe, who have been teaching for me for 14 years, and Lindsay Hopper, who is my General Manager and has also taught for me for 10 years, have been my soldiers, instrumental in keeping this process moving forward. This work is a culmination of my collective knowledge from 44 years of teaching. Without them, this process would have taken twice as long.

Mad respect to them as the fine, outstanding, incredible people and artists they are and I look forward to working with them on many projects in the future.

The best is yet to come.

About the Author

Richard Lawson is what he teaches his students to become: a complete artist practiced in the art and science of Show Business. While his varied career of 55+ years has encompassed a wide range of vocations—award-winning actor, director, teacher, writer, public speaker and drug counselor for the National Basketball Association—Richard's mission has always had a singular focus: To create an acting academy guiding, supporting and empowering individuals to realize their aspirations.

Today, as both a working actor and the founder and Creative Director of the internationally acclaimed Richard Lawson Studios (RLS, launched in 2005), Richard and his team use motivational and cutting-edge technology to impart his holistic approach, which includes traditional scene study, exercises and auditioning classes. This solid foundation, combined with on-camera instruction, filmmaking and business strategy, forms a comprehensive course of study. The approach is based upon moment-to-moment spontaneous work inspired by *Imagination*, passion and purpose.

Richard also extends these time-tested acting techniques to empower non-actors, job seekers, and ambitious individuals to help them achieve their dreams.

Career Highlights

As Richard emphasizes the significance of leading by example, he has always held himself and his career as proof of concept in his teaching methods. A protégé of legendary acting teacher Milton Katselas, Richard joined his mentor's teaching staff in 1980, instructing thousands of students—including many luminaries who are household names—while his acting career flourished.

Richard's first professional acting job was in the national company of *No Place To Be Somebody*.

Some of his more notable theatrical performances included *Ma Rainey's Black Bottom* at the Los Angeles Theatre Center (LATC) and *Streamers* at the Westwood Playhouse (now called the Geffen Playhouse)—both of which received a Drama Critics Award. Other memorable experiences included productions of *Fool For Love* at LATC, *Checkmates* at the Westwood Playhouse, a New York Shakespeare Festival production of *The Mighty Gents*, a New York Manhattan Theater Company world premiere of *The Talented Tenth*, the American premiere of

Hapgood at the Doolittle Theater (now called the Ricardo Montalbán Theatre) in Los Angeles, two different productions of *Othello*—one at the Houston Shakespeare Festival and the other at the Beverly Hills Playhouse (directed by Milton Katselas)—*Visions and Lovers* at the Skylight Theater (also directed by Katselas), and *The Exonerated* at The Actors' Gang Theater in Los Angeles.

Some of Richard's selected films include Steven Spielberg's *Poltergeist*, Walter Hill's *Streets of Fire*, *Stick* with Burt Reynolds, *The Main Event* with Barbra Streisand and Ryan O'Neal, *Coming Home* with Jane Fonda and Jon Voight, *Audrey Rose* with Sir Anthony Hopkins and Marsha Mason, *Wag the Dog* with Robert De Niro and Dustin Hoffman, *How Stella Got Her Groove Back* with Whoopi Goldberg and Angela Bassett, *Guess Who* with Bernie Mac and Ashton Kutcher, *For Colored Girls* with Janet Jackson, Whoopi Goldberg, Thandie Newton, Kerry Washington and Tyler Perry's *Divorce in the Black* with Meagan Good and Debbi Morgan.

A few iconic "Blaxploitation" films from the 1970s include *Scream Blacula Scream*, *Black Fist* (originally titled *Bogard*) and *Sugar Hill*.

Richard was a series regular on *The Days and Nights of Molly Dodd*, *Dynasty*, *Chicago Story*, *The Black Hamptons* and *Beauty in Black*, a Netflix series.

Notable television movies include *The Jericho Mile*, *The Golden Moment*, *Johnnie Mae Gibson: FBI*, *Pandora's Clock* and *Jackie's Back*. Richard has also guest-starred on popular series, including *MacGyver* (his recurring character spun off to a pilot called *The Coltons*), *Wiseguy*, *Amen*, *Parenthood*, *St. Elsewhere*,

Picket Fences, Judging Amy, The Division, NYPD Blue, All of Us, Numb3rs, Real Husbands of Hollywood and *The Ms. Pat Show*.

Richard created the role of Lucas Barnes on the soap opera *All My Children*.

To learn more about Richard and RLS, please visit:
richardlawsonstudios.com

About the Publisher

Legacy Launch Pad is a boutique publishing company that works with entrepreneurs from all over the world.

For more information about Legacy Launch Pad Publishing, go to: www.legacylaunchpadpub.com.

Index

INDEX

End Notes

[1] Science and technology. (n.d.). Oxford Reference. https://www.oxfordreference.com/page/134#:~:text=Science%20encompass es%20the%20systematic%20study,scientific%20knowledge%20for%20pra ctical%20purposes

[2] What is cultural anthropology? - Cultural Anthropology Program (U.S. National Park Service). (n.d.). https://www.nps.gov/orgs/1209/what-is-cultural-anthropology.htm#:~:text=Christopher%20Sittler%20and %20Jim%20Naganashe,the%20past%20and%20the%20present

[3] Dictionary.com | Meanings & Definitions of English Words. (2020). In Dictionary.com. https://www.dictionary.com/browse/event

[4] Dictionary.com | Meanings & Definitions of English Words. (2020b). In Dictionary.com. https://www.dictionary.com/browse/behavior

[5] Dictionary.com | Meanings & Definitions of English Words. (2020c). In Dictionary.com. https://www.dictionary.com/browse/rehearsal

[6] Webster's Dictionary 1828 - Webster's Dictionary 1828 - Imagination. (n.d.). Webster's Dictionary 1828. https://webstersdictionary1828.com/Dictionary/Imagination

[7] Schechter, J. A. (2011). My Story Can Beat Up Your Story!: Ten Ways to Toughen Up Your Screenplay from Opening Hook to Knockout Punch.

[8] Milquetoast. (2024). In Merriam-Webster Dictionary. https://www.merriam-webster.com/dictionary/milquetoast

[9] Publishers, H. (n.d.). The American Heritage Dictionary entry: audition. https://ahdictionary.com/word/search.html?q=audition

[10] Dictionary.com | Meanings & Definitions of English Words. (2021). In Dictionary.com. https://www.dictionary.com/browse/flinch

[11] Roosevelt, T. (1910, May 5). *The Man in the Arena*. Theodore Roosevelt Center. https://www.theodorerooseveltcenter.org/Learn-About-TR/TR-Encyclopedia/Culture-and-Society/Man-in-the-Arena.aspx